
UNSTOPPABLE MONEY 2-IN-1 COLLECTION FOR BUSINESS OWNERS

Essential small business startup and growth strategies to launch, scale, and achieve profitability from day one

Unstoppable Profit Series

S.R. BROWN

Halcyon Enterprise Inc.

Unstoppable Money 2-in-1 Collection for Business Owners

This compilation contains two complete works:

BOOK ONE

How to Make Money in Business Online: Proven Blueprint to Crush It in Online Business

Target Launch Series

Originally published 2025

BOOK TWO

Unstoppable Profit for Business Owners: Proven Strategies to Skyrocket Revenue, Cut Costs & Build a Business That Thrives Without You

Unstoppable Profit Series

Originally published 2025

Published by Halcyon Enterprise Inc.

ISBN: 979-8-9927679-7-1

Disclaimer

The information provided in this book is for educational and informational purposes only. While the author has made every effort to ensure accuracy, the strategies and advice presented are based on the author's research, experience, and opinions. Results may vary depending on individual circumstances, market conditions, and business contexts. This book does not constitute professional business, financial, or legal advice. Readers are encouraged to consult with qualified professionals before making significant business decisions or implementing strategies discussed in this work. The author and publisher assume no responsibility for errors, omissions, or outcomes resulting from the application of information contained herein. Any perceived slight of specific people, companies, or organizations is unintentional.

Introduction: Two Paths to Business Success

Welcome to the Unstoppable Money 2-in-1 Collection for Business Owners

If you're reading this book, you're likely facing one of two critical challenges:

You're ready to launch an online business but need a proven blueprint to avoid costly mistakes and find your profitable path faster.

Or you're already running a business, perhaps for years, but struggling to scale it beyond your personal effort. You're trapped in the day-to-day operations instead of building something that generates unstoppable profit.

This collection addresses both challenges head-on, whether you're starting from scratch or transforming an existing business.

Two Complete Guides, One Comprehensive System

This 2-in-1 collection brings together two complete business guides designed to work together for entrepreneurs at every stage:

Book One: How to Make Money in Business Online provides the foundation for both launching new ventures and discovering fresh revenue streams in established businesses. Whether you're just starting out or you've been running your business for years, you'll discover the criteria for selecting winning business ideas, strategies for evaluating profitable models, and proven techniques for building an online presence that generates real income.

Book Two: Unstoppable Profit for Business Owners takes you deeper into the timeless principles that separate struggling entrepreneurs from those who build lasting wealth, regardless of how long you've been in business. Drawing on battle-tested strategies that have worked for over a century, from PT Barnum's era to today's digital economy, you'll learn how to engineer attention, create customer evangelists, and build systems that scale beyond your personal involvement.

Together, these books form a complete roadmap. They guide you from launching your first online venture to revitalizing an existing business, from generating initial revenue to building an unstoppable profit machine that works without consuming all your time.

Why This Collection Exists

Most business books give you either tactical startup advice or high-level scaling principles, rarely both. But here's the reality: you need both to succeed, whether you're brand new or experienced.

New entrepreneurs need to know how to identify profitable opportunities, validate ideas quickly, and generate first revenue. Experienced business owners need these same skills to discover new revenue streams and pivot when markets shift.

Both new and established businesses need to understand the foundational principles that allow you to scale revenue, build lasting customer relationships, and create a business that doesn't require your constant attention.

This collection bridges that gap for entrepreneurs at any stage.

What You'll Discover

In Book One: How to Make Money in Business Online, you'll learn:

• Online business growth trends you can capitalize on immediately, whether launching new or expanding existing ventures

• Criteria for selecting the perfect online business idea for your specific situation and experience level

• Strategies for evaluating and choosing profitable business models that complement or replace your current income

• How to identify low-hanging fruit and customer pain points that generate revenue quickly

• Essential tools and resources for online business success at any scale

- Proven strategies for growing your online presence and income, even if you're starting with an established offline business

In Book Two: Unstoppable Profit for Business Owners, you'll master:

- Finding your founder-market fit and choosing your strategic position, critical whether you're launching or repositioning

- Smart capital strategies and sustainable growth principles that work for startups and mature businesses alike

- Engineering attention and demand in crowded markets, regardless of your current business stage

- Building customer evangelists who become your best marketing channel

- Developing unbreakable persistence and staying connected to your core business, especially crucial for experienced owners who've drifted from their original vision

- Building an unassailable reputation and maintaining laser focus

- Creating systems that work without you and protecting your strategic advantages

The Timeless Meets the Tactical

What makes this collection unique is how it combines immediate tactical steps with timeless strategic principles. It speaks to both aspiring and established entrepreneurs.

Book One gives you the modern playbook for online business. You get specific steps, tools, and strategies you can implement today, whether you're starting fresh or adding new capabilities to an existing operation. Book Two grounds those tactics in principles that have generated wealth for over a century. Your success won't depend on fleeting trends or algorithm changes. These principles work whether you're in year one or year twenty of your entrepreneurial journey.

Before Steve Jobs was selling a vision from a stage, before Sara Blakely built a billion-dollar brand, before any influencer monetized their personal platform, there was PT Barnum. He faced the same fundamental challenges you face today: sleepless nights wondering if his product would find its market, the weight of payroll when revenue dipped, the constant fight for attention, and the temptation to chase every shiny opportunity.

These challenges don't discriminate based on experience. First-time entrepreneurs and seasoned business owners face them alike.

The principles that built his $300 million fortune (in today's dollars) still work. The attention economy has simply moved from crowded city streets to crowded social media feeds. The trust deficit exists whether you're showcasing "curiosities" or making bold startup claims. The scale challenge remains whether you're managing a traveling circus or a remote team across time zones.

How to Use This Collection

You can read these books in order or jump to the one that addresses your most pressing need:

Start with Book One if you're:

• Launching your first online business

• An established business owner looking for new revenue streams

• Wanting to add online capabilities to your existing offline business

• Needing tactical guidance on tools and strategies for digital expansion

• Ready to break through revenue plateaus with fresh approaches

Start with Book Two if you're:

• Already running a business (new or established) but struggling to scale

• Feeling trapped in day-to-day operations despite years of experience

• Looking to build systems that work without you

• Ready to master the foundational principles of lasting business success

• Seeking to transform your business from a job you own into an asset that generates wealth

However you approach this collection, know that these aren't separate philosophies. They're complementary systems designed to work together for entrepreneurs at every stage of the journey.

A Note on Implementation

This isn't theory. Every principle, strategy, and framework in this collection has been tested in real businesses, both startups and established operations. Book One draws from current online business practices that are generating revenue right now for new entrepreneurs and experienced business owners alike. Book Two expands upon principles that have created wealth across multiple economic eras and technological shifts, regardless of the entrepreneur's experience level.

Your job isn't to consume information passively. It's to implement actively.

Each chapter provides specific action steps, frameworks, and metrics. Use them. Test them in your business. Adapt them to your specific situation, whether you're launching, growing, or transforming. The strategies that work are the ones you actually execute.

Your Journey Starts Here

Whether you're taking the leap into online business for the first time, adding new revenue streams to an established operation, or ready to transform your existing business into an unstoppable profit machine, this collection provides the complete roadmap.

You'll learn how to identify opportunities, validate ideas quickly, generate revenue, build customer evangelists, create scalable systems, and protect your strategic advantages. Everything you need to build a business that creates both wealth and freedom, regardless of where you're starting from.

The principles are timeless. The strategies are proven. They work for new ventures and established businesses alike. The only variable is your willingness to implement them.

Let's get started!

How To Make Money
In Business Online

PROVEN BLUEPRINT TO CRUSH
IT IN ONLINE BUSINESS

TARGET LAUNCH SERIES

S.R. BROWN

Copyright

How to Make Money in Business Online

Copyright © 2025 by Halcyon Enterprise Inc.
    All rights reserved.

No part of this book may be reproduced, distributed, or transmitted in any
    form or by any means, including photocopying, recording, or other electronic
    or mechanical methods, without the prior written permission of the publisher,
    except in the case of brief quotations embodied in critical reviews and
    certain other noncommercial uses permitted by copyright law.

Published by Halcyon Enterprise Inc.

ISBN: 978-0-9835300-2-2

Disclaimer
    The information provided in this book is for educational and informational purposes only. While the author has made every effort to ensure accuracy, the strategies and advice presented are based on the author's research, experience, and opinions. Results may vary depending on individual circumstances, market conditions, and business contexts. This book does not constitute professional business, financial, or legal advice. Readers are encouraged to consult

with qualified professionals before making significant business decisions or implementing strategies discussed in this work. The author and publisher assume no responsibility for errors, omissions, or outcomes resulting from the application of information contained herein. Any perceived slight of specific people, companies, or organizations is unintentional.

How To Make Money In Business Online

Table of Contents - Book 1

Introduction

Introduction

From your first launch to your fifth, **How to Make Money in Business Online** is your blueprint for turning hard work into real profit.

In this book, we will explore the exciting realm of online entrepreneurship, capitalizing on growth trends, and innovative ways of making money.

Our guide will empower you with critical knowledge on evaluating, selecting, and refining your business models, taking into consideration various factors to help you seize lucrative opportunities such as demand, difficulty, and time commitment.

Whether you're just starting out or have been running your business for years, this book is designed to help you break through barriers, find new revenue streams, and achieve unprecedented growth.

In this book, you'll discover:

- Online business growth and trends that you can take advantage of to make money
- Criteria for selecting the perfect online business idea
- Strategies for evaluating and choosing profitable business models
- Tips on setting benchmarks and identifying money-making opportunities
- The importance of defining and aligning your business identity
- How to craft a unique story for maximum profitability
- Ways to uncover low-hanging fruit and identify customer needs

- Proven strategies for growing your online business

This book is about the steps you can take as an entrepreneur, so we don't spend a lot of time citing endless success stories of other entrepreneurs. We will discuss ways your business identity plays a critical role in distinguishing you from your competitors, and we'll discuss how to craft a unique business story and align your actions for optimal profitability.

We also unravel the secrets of spotting low-hanging fruit in your business domain - plus those precious customer pain points that, when solved, can generate significant revenue.

We'll delve into essential techniques for growing your online business, and you'll be inspired by strategies that have been innovated and adapted to help make you money and thrive.

So, if you're an entrepreneur eager to break new ground, maximize profitability, and shape an indomitable online presence, or if you're a seasoned business owner looking to accelerate growth, redefine success, and seize new opportunities, this guide is curated just for you. Get ready to embark on this transformative journey to unleash your business potential. Let's dive in!

Are you ready to take the leap, start your own venture, and make money online? With the rapid growth of online tools and the countless opportunities available, there has never been a better time to dive in. In this ultimate guide to making money in business, we'll explore various online business ideas, share valuable insights on trends, and provide essential tools and resources to help you succeed.

Get ready to embark on an exciting path toward financial freedom and the satisfaction of owning a thriving business.

- Discover the potential of online business and uncover exciting ideas to make money.
- Research demand, evaluate difficulty level & time commitment, and choose tools & resources for success.
- Leverage case studies to learn from successful businesses

how perseverance, innovation, and strategic thinking can help you succeed!

I understand that while listening to this audio version of the book, you might be wondering how you can access the tables, bonus content, and other visual aids. Here's the good news: We've got you covered.

You can find all these resources on our companion website. Simply head over to eLuminateNetwork.com, and you'll find all the visual materials organized by book chapter for easy navigation. Additionally, this site is home to our exclusive bonus content, which I'm sure you'll find beneficial as you progress on your entrepreneurial journey. So, whether you're looking for tables, graphs, or that extra information to push your business forward, remember it's all just a click away.

Happy reading!

Making Money with an Online Business: Overview

The universe of online business is massive and constantly evolving. Whether you're selling your handmade masterpieces on Etsy or dishing out expert advice through online consulting, the sky is the limit.

Though there is more to success online than just getting yourself a reliable internet connection and having a fantastic business idea, we'll explore tactics and strategies that will have you on your way to making money online.

But first, how do you pick the perfect business model for yourself? With many options at your fingertips, it can be daunting. That's what we're going to discuss.

Whether you are a novice entrepreneur embarking on your first business venture or a seasoned business owner with years of experience, The Ultimate Guide to Making Money in Business Online offers practical strategies and insights to help you maximize your

online business profits, making it an invaluable resource for anyone looking to succeed in the digital marketplace.

In this book, we will introduce you to some thrilling online business ideas and help you navigate the factors to weigh in before diving headfirst into your venture or expanding your existing venture.

So, let's jump in and unearth the incredible potential in the digital world.

Growth and Trends

Did you know that the global eCommerce market is expected to reach a staggering $6.5 trillion and that the number of online shoppers is anticipated to reach 2.44 billion by 2025? This means a large and growing market for businesses that sell products or services online.

According to a report by eMarketer, this growth is driven by a number of factors, including the rise of mobile commerce, the growth of social commerce, and the increasing popularity of online shopping among consumers in developing countries.

So, if you're an entrepreneur looking to make money online, there is a massive opportunity for businesses to make money online.

With more people shopping online than ever, there's no better time to start capitalizing on the trends. Plus, the rise of remote work has seen a surge in demand for online courses and services, with millions looking to learn new skills and expand their horizons.

The rapid growth of social media platforms has also opened up new opportunities for making money online. From YouTube channels to Instagram influencers, many people could leverage your personal brands to generate revenue through advertising and affiliate marketing.

According to Forrester Research, social commerce (the buying and selling of products or services through social media platforms like Facebook, Instagram, and Pinterest) will account for 14% of global e-commerce sales in 2025. This represents a whopping 6% increase from 2021.

The potential for success in the online business world is immense, and with the right idea and strategy, you can also reap the rewards.

Trends in Making Money Online

The rise of video content and streaming platforms like TikTok and Twitch has opened up new avenues for entrepreneurs to engage with audiences and monetize content.

Additionally, the demand for online courses and tutoring services continues to grow, offering experts in various fields the opportunity to share their knowledge and generate income.

Another trend gaining momentum is the proliferation of app development and online marketplaces, allowing entrepreneurs to create and sell products or services easily. Online businesses are no longer limited to selling physical products as digital products, subscription services, and even experiences are now on the table.

———

By staying ahead of these trends and adapting to the ever-changing digital landscape, you can position yourself for success in online businesses.

CHAPTER 2

Criteria for Online Business Ideas

Before diving into any business, evaluate your options so you make informed decisions based on factors such as market demand, feasibility, and potential profitability.

In The Ultimate Guide to Making Money In Business Online, we look at four factors that can lead to a higher probability of success — demand, the difficulty level to get started, time commitment, and how long it would take a person to get started.

Considering these criteria, you'll be better equipped to choose the right online business idea that aligns with your skills, interests, and lifestyle.

Online Business Demand

Understanding the demand for your online business idea is paramount to its success. Take, for example, the field of online tutoring, which has experienced a surge in popularity. Science, math, and English are particularly sought-after subjects, presenting lucrative opportunities for entrepreneurs in this domain.

By recognizing and tapping into such high-demand areas, individuals can position their online businesses for greater profitability and long-term viability.

Other high-demand online businesses include SEO consulting and web development, as companies and individuals continuously look for ways to boost their online presence and reach potential customers.

When selecting your online business idea, it's essential to research the market and identify gaps or niches where your skills and expertise can make a difference. By focusing on a specific niche, you can set yourself apart from the competition and cater to a dedicated audience, increasing the chances of success for your online business.

Difficulty Level in Getting Started

The difficulty level of starting an online business varies depending on your chosen business type. For instance, selling services or consulting online may require significant hard work and expertise. On the other hand, starting a print-on-demand business can be relatively easy if you already have designs ready to upload.

Considering the effort and resources required to start and maintain your chosen online business is essential. Be honest with yourself about your capabilities and limitations, and pick a business idea that you can realistically manage and grow over time.

Time Commitment

The time commitment required for online business ideas can also vary greatly. Some businesses, like online tutoring or consulting, may demand more time, especially as you take on more clients.

On the other hand, businesses such as eCommerce or app development may require a more flexible time commitment, allowing you to work on your own schedule.

When evaluating potential online business ideas, you must consider how much time you're willing and able to invest. Be realistic about your availability, and go for a business idea that aligns with your lifestyle and other commitments.

How long will it take a person to get started?

The time it takes to earn money in different online businesses differs greatly. For instance, if you choose to become a freelancer, you can expect to start earning within just a few days of sending out personalized emails and applications.

Conversely, starting an eCommerce business or developing an app may take longer to generate revenue as you'll need to create and market your products or services.

Ultimately, the time it takes to start earning money in an online business depends on the type of business, your skills, and the resources available. By setting clear goals and dedicating time and effort to your chosen business idea, you can start making money online and achieve long-term success.

By considering these criteria, you can narrow down your options and choose the right online business idea for you.

Here are additional tips for selecting an online business idea:

- Think about your skills and interests. What are you good at? What do you enjoy doing? These are the areas where you're most likely to be successful.
- Do your research. Once you have a few ideas, take some time to research the market and see if there's a demand for your product or service.
- Talk to other entrepreneurs. Get advice from people who have already started their own online businesses. They can offer valuable insights and help you avoid common pitfalls.
- Don't be afraid to fail. Everyone fails at some point. The important thing is to learn from your mistakes and keep moving forward.

———

Starting an online business can be a great way to be your own boss and work from home, but it's essential to research and choose the right idea for you. By following these tips, you can increase your chances of success.

CHAPTER 3

Top Online Business Ideas and Revenue Streams

According to a study by the Harvard Business Review, 70% of new businesses fail within the first ten years. One of the main reasons for failure is a lack of profitability.

Indeed, coming up with a great business idea is only half the battle. You also need to be able to execute that idea and generate revenue. That's why it's essential to consider the different revenue streams available to you before making a final decision about your business.

What is the difference between a business idea and revenue streams?

Let's clarify an important distinction that can make or break your success as an entrepreneur: the difference between a business idea and revenue streams. You see, a business idea is the big picture's overarching concept. It's what your business is all about - maybe it's selling handcrafted jewelry, offering professional coaching, or building a digital marketing agency.

On the other hand, revenue streams are the specific ways your business makes money. For example, if you're running that hand-crafted jewelry business, you could sell your products online, at craft shows, or wholesale to retailers - each of these is a different revenue stream.

You might be wondering why you should focus on revenue streams first. The answer is simple: you don't have a sustainable business without revenue. It doesn't matter how great your business idea is if it doesn't generate income. By focusing on your revenue streams first, you ensure that your business idea has the potential to be profitable. You'll be able to determine whether there's a market for your products or services and validate your idea before investing too much time and resources into it.

Understanding your revenue streams also gives you greater control and flexibility. By having multiple revenue streams, you're not putting all your eggs in one basket. If one revenue stream experiences a downturn, others can help offset the loss. Different revenue streams can also appeal to different customer segments, enabling you to reach a broader audience.

So, my advice to any entrepreneur is this: Focus on identifying and developing diverse, sustainable revenue streams first. Your business idea may be the heart of your venture, but your revenue streams are the lifeblood that keeps it alive and thriving.

Why multiple revenue streams?

A study by the Small Business Administration found that businesses that focus on multiple revenue streams are more likely to be successful than those that focus on a single revenue stream.

There are many different ways to generate revenue, and the best approach for you will depend on your specific business model and target market. For example, if you're selling a physical product, you might generate revenue through e-commerce product sales. Meanwhile, you might earn through service plus commission fees if you're providing a service. And if you're creating digital content, you might generate income through advertising or subscription fees.

The key is to choose the correct revenue streams for your business. If you pick the right ones, you could end up with a business that could be more profitable.

Here are a few reasons why it's beneficial for entrepreneurs to consider revenue streams before making a final decision about their business ideas:

- It can help avoid costly mistakes. If you don't consider the different revenue streams available, you could invest a lot of time and money into a business that's not profitable.
- It can help you focus your efforts. Once you know which revenue streams to focus on, you can center your marketing and sales efforts on those areas.
- It can help you grow your business. As your business grows, you may need to add new revenue streams to keep up with demand. Considering different revenue streams from the start prepares you for growth.

Revenue Stream Types

When it comes to making money in business, you can use several strategies. One of the most important decisions you'll make is about your revenue stream and how you want to make money. Many options are available, each with its advantages and disadvantages.

A study by the Kauffman Foundation found that businesses that generate revenue through multiple channels are more likely to grow than those that generate income through a single channel.

Let's look at the different types of revenue streams and discuss the approaches you can use to generate them. Let's also discuss choosing your business's revenue stream and strategy.

So, whether you're just starting or looking to grow your existing business, this section will give you the information you need to make money in business.

Here are some of the different types of revenue streams:

- **Product sales:** This is the most common type of revenue stream. Sell products to customers and generate revenue from the sales.
- **Service fees:** Charge customers for services they provide, like consulting, training, or repairs.
- **Subscription fees:** Charge customers a recurring fee to access products or services. Subscriptions are a

popular way to generate revenue for online content or software businesses.

- **Advertising/Sponsorship revenue:** Sell advertising space on websites or apps to generate income. Also, partner with other businesses to promote your products or services.
- **Licensing revenue:** License intellectual property (e.g., patents, trademarks, and copyrights) to other businesses in exchange for a fee.
- **Affiliate Marketing**: Earn a commission when customers purchase through a link you provide.

- **Digital Downloads/Products:** Digital downloads are electronic versions of products (e.g., music, movies, software, and e-books) that a customer purchases and downloads to a computer or mobile device.
- **Consulting/Coaching:** Consulting is a more formal service typically involving a consultant providing expert advice and guidance on a specific issue or area of expertise. Coaching is a more informal service typically involving a coach working with an individual or team to help them improve your performance.
- **Events/Workshop:** Events can be large or small, formal or informal, lasting for a few hours or several days. Meanwhile, workshops are typically smaller and more focused than events, providing attendees with hands-on training or instruction on a specific topic.
- **Merchandising**: Merchandising includes product placement, store displays, promotional campaigns, and pricing strategies designed to amplify brand presence, elevate customer experience, outperform competitors, and drive sales.
- **Crowdfunding**: Crowdfunding is a form of crowdsourcing and alternative finance for entrepreneurs to raise money for a project or venture.

In a moment, we will take a deeper look at each of these revenue streams and their advantages and disadvantages. Choosing the right proceeds for your business based on your target market, your products or services, and your business goals is essential.

Once you've chosen a revenue stream, you must develop a revenue- generating strategy that includes pricing your products or services, marketing your products or services, and providing customer service.

By following these steps, you can earn and grow your business.

Revenue Streams to Monetize Your Business

There are many ways to monetize a business, from product sales, service fees, advertising, and affiliate marketing to digital products, consulting, and events. The possibilities are endless. But with so many options available, it can be tough to know where to start.

If you're an experienced entrepreneur, you've probably seen firsthand how different revenue streams can impact your business's bottom line. However, it doesn't matter if you are just starting out or are a seasoned veteran, some of the keys to successfully making money in business include:

- Knowing there is no one-size-fits-all approach to monetization. What works for one business may not work for another. That's why choosing the right revenue streams for your business model, market dynamics, and customer needs is important.
- Daring to experiment. The best way to find out what works for your business is to try different things. Don't be afraid to fail. Failure is a part of the learning process.
- Focusing on providing value. The best way to attract and retain customers is to provide value. If you can do that, they'll be more likely to pay for your products and services.

So, how do you discern the right revenue stream for you? Here are a few things to consider:

- Your target market. Who do you want to serve? Who are you trying to reach? What are your needs and wants?
- Your products or services. What do you want to offer? How can you make it more valuable to your customers?
- Your business goals. What do you want to achieve with your business? How can revenue streams help you reach your goals?

Once you've considered these factors, you can explore different revenue streams.

The most important thing is to start somewhere. Don't wait for the perfect opportunity. The best way to learn is by doing. So, get out there and start experimenting. The sooner you start, the sooner you'll find the right proceeds for your business.

The key to successful monetization is identifying these revenue streams and strategically aligning them with your business model, market dynamics, and customer needs.

1. Product Sales

Turn inventory into income through direct sales

Product sales:selling physical or digital products directly to customers are one of the most traditional revenue streams. According to Statista, global retail e-commerce sales are expected to reach $6.35 trillion by 2027, representing an annual growth rate of 11.51% from 2023 to 2027.

When considering product sales, entrepreneurs must contemplate factors such as product demand, pricing strategy, production, distribution costs, and competition.

Kickstarting your business involves key steps. Identify in-demand products, understand your potential customers, and pick high-margin products for early profits. Next, we'll cover a brief overview of getting started and then dive into some specific techniques you can use to find trending products.

Here are the core steps to getting started:

1. **Do your research.** The first step is to do your research and identify products that are in high demand. You can use various tools to do this, such as Google Trends, Amazon Best Sellers, and social media. More on these later.

2. **Consider your target market.** Once you've identified some potential products, you need to consider your target market. Who are you selling to? What are your needs and wants? Once you understand your target market, you can better identify products they are likely interested in.

3. **Look for products with high margins.** Entrepreneurs should focus on high-margin products to maximize profits. The higher the margin, the more money the entrepreneur makes on each sale.

4. **Find a supplier.** Once you've found a product you want to sell, you must find a supplier. There are many ways to do so, such as online directories, trade shows, and networking.

5. **Set up your store.** Once you've found a supplier, you must set up your online or offline store. If you're selling online, choose a platform like Shopify or WooCommerce. You must find a location and set up your inventory if you're selling offline.

6. **Market your product.** Start marketing your product once you've set up your store. You can do this through various channels, such as social media, search engine optimization, and paid advertising.

Finding Products in High Demand

One of the most valuable things you can do to increase your chances of finding a highly-demanded product to sell is to look for what is trending, unique, and easy to sell.

Look for products that are trending:

You can use Google Trends to see which products are trending. Research can give you an idea of what products are in high demand and likely to sell well.

- Look for products trending upward, which means that interest in the product is increasing, which is a good indication that it is in high demand.
- Look for products with a high search volume, which indicates that many people are searching for the product, which is another good sign that it is in high demand.
- Look for relevant products to your target market and that reflect something your ideal customer is likely to buy.

4 Search Criteria to Use in Google Trends

Here are a few examples of what to search for to find a product using Google Trends:

1. Product categories:

You can search for broad product categories, such as "clothing," "electronics," or "home goods."

2. Specific products:

You can also search for specific products, such as "iPhone," "Nike shoes," or "Samsung TV" to find popular product brands that you might be able to sell for a profit.

3. Keywords:

Another option is to look up keywords related to the products you're interested in selling. For example, if you're considering selling clothing, you could search for keywords like "fashion," "style," or "trends."

4. Events:

You can also search for events such as "Black Friday," "Cyber Monday," or "Christmas" to help you find products that are in high demand during these times.

Trends change quickly, so staying up-to-date on the latest trends is important. If you can find a product that is trending, you're more likely to be able to sell it for a profit.

Finding products that will earn you money

Being creative is one of the most overlooked tips that can help you succeed in the product and e-commerce landscape. Don't be afraid to think outside the box when searching for products. You might be surprised at what you find.

Look for products that solve problems:

People are always looking for products to make their lives easier or solve problems. If you can find one that does this, you will likely find a market for it. In a moment, we'll explore this strategy more and see how it can help you earn money.

Look for unique or unusual products:

People are often drawn to products that are unique or unusual. If you can find something that stands out from the competition, you're more likely to succeed.

Look for products that are in high demand:

If you can find a product that is in high demand, you're more likely to be able to sell it for a profit.

Here are some specific examples of products that you might find if you're creative:

- A product that helps people save time, such as a meal delivery service or a personal assistant app.
- A product that solves a problem, such as one that helps people sleep better or lose weight.
- A unique or unusual product, such as one made from recycled materials or designed to support a cause.
- A product in high demand, such as one related to a popular TV show or used by celebrities.
- A trending product, such as one related to a current event or used by influencers.

By being creative, you can increase your chances of finding products in high demand and with a greater probability for you to sell for a profit.

Look for products that are easy to sell:

You want to choose a product that is easy to sell. Search for something people are already looking for and willing to pay for.

By following these tips, you can increase your chances of finding a product to sell that is in high demand and profitable.

2. Service Fees

Generate recurring revenue through expertise and subscriptions

Let's look at service fees as a viable strategy for new entrepreneurs to make money and highlight the factors that make this approach more effective than alternative revenue streams.

Service fees can be a substantial source of revenue for businesses that provide services instead of goods. This could include anything from a digital marketing agency's consulting fee to a software-as-a-service (SaaS) platform subscription fee.

According to Transparency Market Research, the global SaaS market is projected to $307.87 billion by 2028. This is up from $220.21 billion in 2022. Pricing strategy, the value provided, and competition are crucial considerations when setting your service fees.

Getting Started in Service Fees: Finding Your Niche

The first step in starting a service-based business is finding your niche. To do this, consider the following factors:

1. **Market demand:** Research the market to identify services with high demand and low competition. Look for trends and consumer needs that are not being met by existing service providers.
2. **Profit margins:** Choose a service with healthy profit margins, ensuring that you can cover expenses and still make a profit.
3. **Scalability:** Opt for a service that allows for growth and expansion over time. This means selecting a service that can be easily scaled up as your business grows.

By carefully considering these factors, you can ensure that you have chosen a viable service to offer—one that has the potential to generate consistent revenue.

Why Customization Is an Advantage for Service Fee Models

Service fees offer several advantages over alternative revenue streams, such as product sales or affiliate marketing. These advantages include:

4. **Customization:** With service-based businesses, you can tailor your offerings to meet the specific needs of your clients, making it easier to stand out from competitors and build long-term client relationships.
   1. **Lower overhead costs:** In many cases, service-based businesses have lower overhead costs than product-based businesses because they don't require as much inventory or storage space.
   2. **Higher scalability:** Service-based businesses often have better scalability, allowing for rapid growth when managed effectively.

Service Fee Types

Let's dive into a few of the service fee models that you can implement as an entrepreneur to generate more revenue for your business:

1. **Flat Fee Model:**

This is a simple, straightforward pricing structure where you charge a single fixed fee for a specific service. This model is clear and easy for customers to understand. For example, a graphic designer might charge $500 for a logo design. According to a survey by The Freelancer by Contently, 37% of freelancers prefer a flat fee model for its simplicity and reliability.

2. **Hourly Rate Model:**

This model involves charging customers based on the number of hours worked. It's often used in consulting, freelancing, and other professional services. The U.S. Bureau of Labor Statistics reported in 2022 that the average hourly wage for consultants was $40.52. However, rates can significantly vary based on industry, expertise, and location.

3. **Subscription or Retainer Model:**

In this model, customers pay a recurring fee, typically monthly or annually, to have continual access to a service. This model provides predictable revenue and encourages customer loyalty. According to Zuora's Subscription Economy Index, subscription businesses grew revenues about five times faster than S&P 500 company revenues (18.2% versus 3.6%) from 2012 to 2019.

4. **Tiered Pricing Model:**

This model offers different levels of service at various price points. For example, a software-as-a-service (SaaS) company might offer a basic plan, a pro plan, and an enterprise plan, each with different features and benefits. According to a study by Price Intelligently, tiered pricing increases revenue by 25-75%.

5. **Value-Based Model:**

In this model, pricing is based on the perceived or estimated value of the results your service will bring to the customer rather than the cost of the service itself. A study by the Professional Pricing Society found that value-based pricing can increase profits by 15% compared to cost-plus pricing models.

6. **Performance or Contingency-Based Model:**

With this model, fees are based on achieving specific results or milestones. According to a study by the World Bank, performance-based contracts have resulted in efficiency gains of 10-30% in various public sector domains.

The performance-based or contingency fee model, also known as a success fee model, is a pricing structure where a service provider is compensated only once specific results are achieved. This means payment is contingent upon the successful delivery of agreed-upon outcomes, milestones, or performance indicators.

For example, a marketing agency might only get paid once it attains certain key performance indicators (KPIs), such as generating a certain number of leads, achieving a specific conversion rate, or increasing website traffic by a certain percentage. A real estate agent, on the other hand, would receive a percentage of the property's sale price only once the house is sold.

The success fee model aligns the service provider's and the client's interests, as both parties have a stake in achieving the desired outcome. This model can also provide an added layer of reassurance to clients as they are not required to pay unless the service yields positive results.

However, there are potential challenges with this model. The service provider assumes more risk and needs to be confident they can deliver the agreed-upon results. It also requires clear communication and agreement on what constitutes "success" to ensure both parties are coordinated.

Data on the success fee model is sparse as it's highly dependent on the specific industry and the nature of the agreement between the service provider and the client. However, a report by Consultancy.org suggests that success fee arrangements are becoming more prevalent in consulting sectors, where clients increasingly prefer 'skin-in-the-game' commitments from your consultants.

As an entrepreneur, it's crucial to understand your market, your value proposition, and your customer's needs and preferences when choosing a service fee model. Different frameworks may be more suitable for different services, industries, and customer segments, so it's wise to test and refine your pricing strategy over time.

Tips and Techniques for Successfully Selling Your Services

Now that you've chosen a service and understand the advantages of service fees, let's discuss how to sell your services effectively. Below are some tips and techniques that will help you maximize sales:

1. **Use multiple marketing channels:** Utilize both digital and traditional marketing channels to reach a wider audience. These can include social media advertising, email marketing, content marketing, and even print ads or trade shows.
2. **Identify key target customer segments:** Understand who your ideal customers are, your needs, and your pain points. This will allow you to tailor your marketing messages to resonate with them more effectively.
3. **Establish a strong value proposition:** Clearly communicate the benefits of your service and what sets it apart from that of y our competitors. A compelling value proposition will make it easier for potential clients to understand why they should choose your service.

Remember, our focus is not on sales principles but rather on the viability to make money in a service business. To succeed in selling your services, it's essential to:

1. **Consistently follow up:** Regularly engage with prospects and clients to build relationships and keep your service top of mind.
2. **Build a strong pipeline:** Continuously add new leads to your sales funnel to ensure a steady flow of potential clients.
3. **Use data to improve conversions:** Analyze your sales data to identify areas for improvement, such as

optimizing your sales process or refining your marketing strategy.

The Benefits of Service Fees for Sustainable Business Growth

In conclusion, service fees offer a viable strategy for achieving sustainable growth in business. By finding the right niche, leveraging effective marketing channels, and focusing on consistency and continuous improvement, entrepreneurs can create a thriving service-based business.

Remember the key takeaways:

- Choose a service with high demand, healthy profit margins, and scalability.
- Utilize multiple marketing channels to maximize sales.
- Consistently follow up and build a strong pipeline.
- Use data to continuously improve conversions.

By leveraging these insights, aspiring entrepreneurs can set themselves up for success with service fees as their primary revenue stream. So go forth, and conquer the world of service-based businesses!

3. Advertising/Sponsorship

Monetize your audience reach and influence

Businesses with a large audience or significant web traffic can monetize through advertising or sponsorships. This includes hosting ads on your website or getting sponsored by a company in exchange for promoting your product or service. According to eMarketer, digital ad spending worldwide is expected to reach $835.82 billion by 2026.

Let's look at advertising and sponsorships as viable strategies for new entrepreneurs to make money.

Getting Started in Advertising/Sponsorship: Finding Your Niche

The first step in starting an advertising/sponsorship-based business is finding your niche. To do this, consider the following factors:

1. **Market demand:** Research the market to identify industries with high demand for advertising and sponsorship opportunities. In 2020, global ad spending reached $590 billion, indicating ample opportunities for entrepreneurs (Statista).
2. **Profit margins:** Choose a niche with healthy profit margins, ensuring you can cover expenses and still make a profit.
3. **Scalability:** Opt for a niche that allows for growth and expansion over time. This means selecting industries with a growing audience and increasing advertising budgets.

By carefully considering these factors, you can ensure that you have chosen a viable niche to tap into—one that has the potential to generate consistent revenue.

Why Advertising/Sponsorship Is More Effective Than Alternative Revenue Streams

Advertising and sponsorship offer several advantages over alternative revenue streams, such as product sales or service fees. These advantages include:

1. **Passive income:** With advertising and sponsorships, you can generate passive income as advertisers pay for ad placements or sponsorships without constant management.
2. **Lower overhead costs:** In many cases, advertising/sponsorship- based businesses have lower

overhead costs than product or service-based businesses because they don't require inventory, storage space, or specialized training.

3. **Higher scalability:** Advertising/sponsorship-based businesses often have better scalability, allowing for rapid growth when managed effectively.

Tips and Techniques for Successfully Monetizing Advertising/Sponsorships

Now that you've chosen a niche and understand the advantages of advertising and sponsorships, let's discuss how to monetize your platform effectively. Below are some tips and techniques that will help you maximize revenue:

1. **Use multiple marketing channels:** Utilize both digital and traditional marketing channels to reach a wider audience. According to eMarketer, global digital ad spending reached $389 billion in 2021, emphasizing the importance of online marketing.

2. **Identify key target customer segments:** Understand who your ideal advertisers and sponsors are, your needs, and your pain points. Doing so will allow you to tailor your platform to resonate with them more effectively.

3. **Cement a robust value proposition**: Communicate the perks of advertising or sponsoring via your platform and how it stands out from rivals. A persuasive value proposition simplifies the decision-making process for potential advertisers and sponsors by showcasing why your platform is the ideal choice.

For instance, if you run a podcast with a niche audience in the health and wellness sector, your value proposition might be that advertisers can precisely target health-conscious consumers who are already interested and invested in their product category, thereby leading to higher conversion rates compared to more generalized platforms.

To succeed in advertising and sponsorships, there are three core essentials:

1. **Building a high-value audience:**

Advertising and sponsorship revenue typically correlate with the size and quality of the audience you can reach. Focusing on building an engaged audience that is of interest to advertisers or sponsors is vital. This audience could be on a blog, YouTube channel, podcast, or social media platform and should be targeted towards a specific niche to maximize value. For instance, a tech blog that has an audience of tech-savvy, high-income individuals would be appealing to tech brands.

2. **Promote the benefits:**

It's crucial to clearly articulate to potential advertisers or sponsors the unique benefits they'll gain from partnering with you. This can involve audience demographics, successful past partnerships, or your unique positioning within your market. For instance, a popular health and wellness podcast might offer sponsors targeted access to health-conscious consumers, a benefit that can be quantified by past successful campaigns with similar brands.

3. **Effective ad or sponsorship packages:**

Offering flexible, value-added sponsorship or advertising packages can increase your attractiveness to potential partners. These packages might include various ad placements (banner ads, sponsored posts, podcast mentions), social media shout-outs, email marketing inclusion, or event sponsorship opportunities.

A diverse range of offerings can cater to the varied needs of potential advertisers, from those looking for brand visibility to those seeking direct customer conversions. Providing clear information on pricing, audience reach, and expected outcomes can facilitate the decision- making process for potential sponsors.

The Benefits of Advertising/Sponsorship for Sustainable Business Growth

Advertising and sponsorship offer a viable strategy for achieving sustainable growth in business. By finding the right niche, leveraging effective marketing channels, and focusing on consistency and continuous improvement, entrepreneurs can create a thriving advertising/sponsorship-based business.

Remember the key takeaways:

- Choose a niche with high demand, healthy profit margins, and scalability
- Utilize multiple marketing channels to maximize revenue
- Consistently follow up and build a strong pipeline
- Use data to continuously improve conversions

4. Affiliate Marketing

Turn recommendations into passive income by promoting products you trust

With affiliate marketing, businesses promote other companies' products or services and earn a commission on any sales made through your referral. According to Statista, affiliate marketing spending in the United States is expected to reach $12.4 billion by 2026. Also, the growth of e-commerce is creating new opportunities for affiliate marketers and is expected to account for 14.3% of all retail sales in the United States by 2026. The global affiliate marketing market is rapidly growing, reaching $27.78 billion by 2027.

Choosing the right products that align with your audience's interests is vital to successful affiliate marketing.

Affiliate Marketing To Make Money

Affiliate marketing is a powerful strategy for entrepreneurs seeking to monetize their platforms, such as blogs, YouTube channels, or social media accounts. As an affiliate marketer, you promote other companies' products or services and earn a commission on every sale made through your unique affiliate link.

Affiliate marketing is a low-risk model because you don't need to create, store, or ship products, nor deal with customer service. Plus, the income potential is significant, with many affiliate programs offering generous commission rates, from Amazon's up to 10% to software companies offering up to 30%. It's an excellent opportunity for entrepreneurs who have built an audience and seek ways to generate income while providing valuable product recommendations to their followers.

Why is affiliate marketing on the rise?

There are several factors driving the growth of affiliate marketing, including:

- **The rise of e-commerce:** E-commerce has made it easier for businesses to reach a global audience, and affiliate marketing is a cost-effective way to reach this audience.
- **The growth of social media:** Social media has made it easier for businesses to connect with potential customers, and affiliate marketing can leverage this connection to generate sales.
- **The increasing popularity of influencer marketing:** Influencer marketing refers to affiliate marketing that involves partnering with influencers to promote a product or service. Influencer marketing has

become increasingly popular as businesses have found it an effective way to reach a targeted audience.

If you are considering using affiliate marketing to promote your business, you should keep a few things in mind:

- **Choose the right affiliates:** When choosing affiliates, picking those with a large following and who are relevant to your target market is vital.
- **Set clear goals:** It is essential to set clear goals for your affiliate marketing campaign, such as increasing website traffic, generating leads, or driving sales.
- **Track your results:** It is crucial to track the results of your affiliate marketing campaign to see what is working and what is not.

By following these tips, you can increase your chances of success with affiliate marketing.

Getting Started in Affiliate Marketing: Finding the Right Niche

The first step in starting an affiliate marketing business is finding your niche. To do this, consider the following factors:

- **Market demand:** Research the market to identify niches with high demand and low competition niches. In 2020, the global affiliate marketing industry was worth $12 billion, indicating ample opportunities for entrepreneurs (Statista).
- **Profit margins:** Choose a niche with healthy commission rates, ensuring you can cover expenses and still make a profit.
- **Scalability:** Opt for a niche allowing growth and expansion over time. This means selecting industries with a growing audience and increasing online presence.

By carefully considering these details, you can ensure that you have chosen a viable niche to tap into—one that has the potential to generate consistent revenue.

Why Affiliate Marketing Is More Effective Than Alternative Revenue Streams

Affiliate marketing offers several advantages over alternative revenue streams, such as product sales or service fees. These advantages include:

- **Passive income:** With affiliate marketing, you can generate passive income as advertisers pay commissions for referred sales or leads without the need for constant management.
- **Lower overhead costs:** In many cases, affiliate marketing businesses have lower overhead costs than product or service-based businesses because they don't require inventory, storage space, or specialized training.
- **Higher scalability:** As mentioned earlier, affiliate marketing businesses often have better scalability, allowing for rapid growth when managed effectively.

Tips and Techniques for Successfully Selling Products Through Affiliate Marketing

Now that you've chosen a niche and understand the advantages of affiliate marketing, let's discuss how to sell products effectively through this strategy. Below are some tips and techniques that will help you maximize sales:

1. **Use multiple marketing channels:** Utilize both digital and traditional marketing channels to reach a wider audience. According to eMarketer, global digital ad spending reached $389 billion in 2021, emphasizing the importance of online marketing.

2. **Identify key target customer segments:** Understand who your ideal customers are, your needs, and your pain points. This will allow you to tailor your marketing messages to resonate with them more effectively.

3. **Develop a persuasive value proposition:** Clearly and persuasively lay out the advantages of the products you're advocating for and what differentiates them from the competition. A strong value proposition simplifies the purchasing decision for potential customers by underlining why the products you endorse are the optimal choice.

For instance, if you're promoting a particular brand of eco-friendly athletic wear, your value proposition might be that these garments are not only high-performing and stylish, but also sustainably produced and biodegradable. This provides potential customers with more than just a product; it aligns with their values and contributes to their broader goals of living a sustainable lifestyle. This unique combination of product features and benefits forms a powerful value proposition that's likely to resonate with your target customers.

5. Digital Downloads/Products

Create once, sell repeatedly with scalable assets

Selling digital downloads or products like ebooks, online courses, software, or digital art constitutes another revenue stream. The global e-learning market size is projected to reach $375.8 billion by 2026, according to Fortune Business Insights, showcasing the potential of selling digital educational products. The digital product should provide value, and its creation and delivery costs should be taken into account.

Starting With Digital Download Products: Finding Your Niche

When starting with digital download products, the first step is to find a product that resonates with your interests and expertise. This could be an ebook, online course, software, or any other digital content that can be easily downloaded by customers. Here are some factors to consider when selecting a product:

1. **Market demand:** Research your target market to identify trends and areas with high demand but relatively low competition.
2. **Expertise:** Choose a product in which you have knowledge and experience, making it easier to create high-quality content and engage with your audience.

3. **Scalability:** Opt for products that can be easily scaled and updated as your business grows.

Here are some examples of digital downloads that make the most money:

- **Ebooks** - Digital books offer exceptional profit margins with minimal production costs. While mainstream ebooks average $10-$20, specialized guides and professional resources can command $50-$200 or more, depending on the niche and value provided.
- **Music** - Individual tracks typically sell for $0.99-$1.29, but artists can maximize revenue through albums ($10-$15) and exclusive content bundles. Licensing opportunities for commercial use can generate significantly higher returns.
- **Videos** - From tutorials to entertainment, videos range from $5-$20 for individual purchases. Premium video series, masterclasses, and licensed content for businesses can sell for $100-$500 or more.

- **Software** - Software products offer scalable income through one-time purchases ($50-$500) or subscription models. Specialized business tools and enterprise solutions can generate thousands in recurring revenue per customer.
- **Online Courses** - Among the most lucrative digital products, courses typically range from $100-$500 for comprehensive programs. High-ticket courses in specialized fields like business, technology, and professional development regularly sell for $1,000-$5,000+, with some premium programs exceeding $10,000.

These are just a few examples of digital downloads that can make a lot of money. The specific type of digital download that will make the most money for you will depend on your target market and expertise.

Here are some tips for creating digital downloads that will sell well:

- Create high-quality content: Your digital downloads should be high-quality and valuable to your target market. If your content is not good, people will not be willing to pay for it.
- Price your digital downloads competitively: Your digital downloads should be priced competitively with similar products on the market. If your prices are too high, people will not buy them.
- Market your digital downloads effectively: You need to market your digital downloads effectively in order to reach your target market and generate sales. There are a number of ways to do so, such as through social media, search engine optimization (SEO), and email marketing.

By following these tips, you can increase your chances of success in selling digital downloads.

Why digital download products?

Digital download products offer several advantages over traditional revenue streams, making them an attractive option for new entrepreneurs. Some of these benefits include:

- **Lower upfront investment:** Creating digital products requires less capital compared to physical products, allowing you to test the market without significant financial risk.
- **Higher profit margins:** Since there are no manufacturing, storage, or shipping costs, digital products generally yield higher profit margins.
- **Global reach:** Digital products can be sold anywhere in the world, expanding your potential customer base.
- **Automation:** Once your product is created and set up, sales can be automated, freeing up time for other aspects of your business.

Tips and Techniques for Successfully Selling Digital Download Products

To maximize your success in selling digital download products, consider the following tips and techniques:

- **Marketing channels:** Utilize both digital and traditional marketing channels to reach your target audience. Social media, email marketing, content marketing, and search engine optimization (SEO) are highly effective digital channels, while networking events, workshops, and print advertising can supplement your online efforts.
- **Target customer segments:** Identify key target customer segments and tailor your marketing campaigns to address your specific needs and preferences. This will increase the likelihood of conversions and boost sales.

- **Value proposition:** Explicitly convey the unique value of your digital download to potential customers, emphasizing the specific benefits they can derive and the challenges it will help them overcome.
- For instance, if you're offering a downloadable e-book on "10 Steps to Mastering Digital Marketing," your value proposition could focus on how the book simplifies complex concepts, offers practical and easy-to-follow steps, and provides the tools and strategies needed to boost online visibility, attract more customers, and ultimately grow their business. This potent blend of benefits addresses the needs of your target customers - individuals or small businesses struggling with digital marketing - and demonstrates the distinct value of your downloadable product.

- **Follow-up:** Consistent follow-up is essential for building relationships with potential clients and converting leads into sales. Use email sequences, remarketing, and personal connections to keep your product top-of-mind.
- **Strong pipeline:** Build a strong pipeline of prospects by continuously generating leads through various marketing channels and nurturing them through your sales funnel.
- **Data-driven improvements:** Continuously analyze your sales data to identify areas for improvement and optimize your marketing strategies, targeting, and product offerings.

6. Consulting/Coaching

Transform your knowledge into high-value client relationships

For those with expertise in a specific field, offering consulting or coaching services can be a lucrative source of income. According to a report by IBISWorld, the business coaching industry in the US was worth \$11.6 billion in 2019. The value provided, the demand for the expertise, and the cost involved in delivering the service should always be considered.

Consulting vs. Coaching

Consulting is a more formal service that typically involves a consultant providing expert advice and guidance on a specific issue or area of expertise. Consultants typically have a deep understanding of a particular industry or field and use this knowledge to help their clients solve problems and achieve their goals.

Meanwhile, coaching is a more informal service that typically involves a coach working with an individual or team to help them improve their performance. Coaches usually have experience in the field they are coaching in and use it to help their clients develop new skills, overcome challenges, and achieve their goals.

Starting With Consulting or Coaching: Finding Your Niche

When starting consulting or coaching, the first step is finding a niche that resonates with your interests and expertise. This could be business coaching, career consulting, wellness coaching, or any other area where you can provide valuable guidance and support to clients. Here are some factors to consider when selecting a niche:

- **Market demand:** Research your target market to identify trends and areas with high demand but relatively low competition.
- **Expertise:** Choose a niche in which you have knowledge and experience, making it easier to create high-quality content and engage with your audience.
- **Scalability:** Opt for niches that can be easily scaled and updated as your business grows.

Why Consulting or Coaching Outshines Alternative Revenue Streams

Consulting or coaching offers several advantages over traditional revenue streams, making them an attractive option for entrepreneurs. Some of these benefits include:

- **Lower upfront investment:** Starting a consulting or coaching business requires less capital, usually compared to physical products, allowing you to test the market without significant financial risk.
- **Higher profit margins:** Since there are no manufacturing, storage, or shipping costs, consulting or coaching services generally yield higher profit margins.
- **Global reach:** Consulting or coaching services can be delivered anywhere worldwide, expanding your potential customer base.
- **Flexibility:** You can offer your services in-person, over the phone, or through video conferencing, providing flexibility for you and your clients.

Tips and Techniques for Successfully Selling Consulting or Coaching Services

To maximize your success in selling consulting or coaching services, consider the following tips and techniques:

- **Marketing channels:** Utilize digital and traditional marketing channels to reach your target audience. Social media, email marketing, content marketing, and search engine optimization (SEO) are highly effective digital channels, while networking events, workshops, and print advertising can supplement your online efforts.
- **Target customer segments:** Identify key target customer segments and tailor your marketing campaigns

to address your specific needs and preferences. This will increase the likelihood of conversions and boost sales.

- **Articulate your compelling value proposition:** Clearly convey the unique benefits of your services to prospective customers, centering on the gains they can achieve and the difficulties you can assist in resolving.

For example, if you're a career coach, your value proposition could emphasize how your services provide personalized career strategies, improve job interview skills, and aid in creating compelling resumes. The key benefits - increasing the chances of landing their dream jobs and overcoming career stagnation - directly address your target customers' needs. This clear articulation of value demonstrates how your career coaching services are a solution to their career-related challenges.

- **Follow-up:** Consistent follow-up is essential for building relationships with potential clients and converting leads into sales. Use email sequences, remarketing, and personal connections to keep your services top-of-mind.
- **Strong pipeline:** Build a strong pipeline of prospects by continuously generating leads through various marketing channels and nurturing them through your sales funnel.
- **Data-driven improvements:** Continuously analyze your sales data to identify areas for improvement and optimize your marketing strategies, targeting, and service offerings.

You can create a thriving business built on consulting or coaching services by carefully selecting a niche, leveraging effective marketing channels, and employing data-driven decision-making. Remember that consistency and continuous improvement are critical to executing this strategy successfully.

7. Events/Workshops

Transform your knowledge into high-value client relationships

Businesses can host events, webinars, or workshops to generate revenue. This could be particularly profitable for businesses with expertise in a high-demand area. Grand View Research projects the global e-learning market, which includes online workshops, will reach $1.1 trillion by 2027. These events should offer valuable insights or skills, and venue or platform costs, marketing, and time investment should be evaluated.

Starting With Events and Workshops: Finding Your Niche

When starting in events and workshops, the first step is to find a niche that resonates with your interests and expertise. This could be business workshops, personal development seminars, wellness retreats, or any other area where you can provide valuable experiences and knowledge to attendees. Here are some factors to consider when selecting a niche:

- **Market demand:** Research your target market to identify trends and areas with high demand but relatively low competition.
- **Expertise:** Choose a niche in which you have knowledge and experience, making it easier to create engaging and informative events and workshops.
- **Scalability:** Opt for niches that can be easily scaled and updated as your business grows.

Why Events and Workshops Outshine Alternative Revenue Streams

Events and workshops offer several advantages over traditional revenue streams, making them an attractive option for entrepreneurs. Some of these benefits include:

- **Lower upfront investment:** Organizing events and workshops usually requires less capital than physical products, allowing you to test the market without significant financial risk.
- **Higher profit margins:** Since there are no manufacturing, storage, or shipping costs, events and workshops generally yield higher profit margins.
- **Global reach:** Host events and workshops worldwide, expanding your potential customer base.
- **Networking opportunities:** Hosting events and workshops provides excellent networking opportunities for you and your attendees, helping grow your business and create lasting connections.

Tips and Techniques for Successfully Selling Events and Workshops

To maximize your success in organizing and selling events and workshops, consider the following tips and techniques:

- Marketing channels: Utilize digital and traditional marketing channels to reach your target audience. Social media, email marketing, content marketing, and search engine optimization (SEO) are highly effective digital channels, while networking events, workshops, and print advertising can supplement your online efforts.
- Target customer segments: Identify key target customer segments and tailor your marketing campaigns to address your specific needs and preferences. This will increase the likelihood of conversions and boost attendance.
- Value proposition: Clearly convey the unique benefits of your events and workshops to potential attendees,

focusing on the advantages they will acquire and the issues you can address.

For example, if you're hosting a financial literacy workshop, your value proposition might highlight how attendees can gain a strong understanding of personal finance, budgeting, and investment basics. The key benefits - financial empowerment, money management skills, and understanding of investments - directly target your prospective attendees' needs. This explicit expression of value shows that attending your workshop is a practical solution to their financial challenges.

8. Subscription-Based Models

Create steady cash flow through loyal member subscriptions

A subscription-based business model charges customers a recurring fee (usually monthly or yearly) to access a product or service. This model can be particularly effective for businesses offering digital services, software, or media. Subscription models can generate predictable, recurring revenue and increase customer retention. According to a report by Grand View Research, the global video streaming market, a typical subscription-based industry, is projected to hit $184.3 billion by 2027.

Embracing Subscription-Based Models as a Profitable Strategy for Entrepreneurs

According to a report by McKinsey & Company, the subscription e-commerce market has grown by more than 100% annually since 2013, with the largest retailers generating over $2.6 billion in sales in 2016, up from $57 million in 2011.

Why Choose a Subscription-Based Model?

Subscription-based models offer several advantages over traditional one-time purchase measures, making them an attractive option for entrepreneurs. Some of these benefits include:

- **Predictable revenue:** Subscriptions provide a steady income stream, allowing entrepreneurs to forecast their revenue better and make informed decisions about investments and growth.
- **Increased customer retention:** Subscription models encourage long-term customer relationships, leading to higher retention rates and lower acquisition costs.
- **Enhanced customer insights:** By tracking customer behavior and preferences over time, entrepreneurs can gain valuable insights into their target audience, enabling them to create tailored offerings and improve customer satisfaction.
- **Scalability:** Subscription-based businesses can quickly scale as they typically require less upfront investment in inventory and infrastructure than traditional models.

Subscription-Based Models Examples

Here are some specific examples of subscription-based models that make the most money:

Streaming services: Streaming services like Netflix, Hulu, and Spotify are not precisely within reach for entrepreneurs to develop. These services offer a wide variety of content, including movies, TV shows, music, and podcasts, for a monthly fee.

So, what exactly is a streaming service model that is more obtainable? There are many different types of streaming services that an entrepreneur can start now. Here are a few ideas:

- **A music streaming service:** This type of service allows users to listen to music on demand.

Entrepreneurs could create their music library or partner with other music streaming services to provide content.

- **A video streaming service:** With this type of service, users can watch movies and TV shows on demand. You could create a video library or partner with other streaming services to provide content.
- **A gaming streaming service:** This type of service enables users to play video games on demand. As with a video streaming service, you could create your gaming library or partner with other gaming streaming services to provide content.

A live streaming service allows users to watch live events, such as concerts, sporting events, and talk shows. You could create your own live-streaming platform or partner with other live-streaming services to provide content.

Software as a service (SaaS): SaaS is a subscription-based model where businesses pay a monthly fee to access cloud-based software applications.

- **Memberships:** Memberships are another popular subscription-based model. Businesses offer a variety of benefits to members, such as discounts, early access to products, and exclusive content.
- **Courses:** Courses are a popular subscription-based model for businesses that offer online courses. Businesses charge a monthly fee for access to your courses, which can cover various topics, such as business, marketing, and personal development.
- **Software updates:** Businesses can also generate revenue through subscription-based software updates, allowing them to generate additional revenue from customers who have already purchased their software.

These are just a few subscription-based models that can make much money. The subscription-based model that will make the most money depends on your target market and business model.

Here are some tips for creating a subscription-based model that will be successful:

- **Offer a valuable product or service:** Your subscription- based model should offer a valuable product or service to your target market. If your product or service is not valuable, people will not be willing to pay for it.
- **Set a fair price:** Your subscription price should be reasonable and competitive with similar products or services. If it is too high, people will not subscribe.
- **Make it easy to sign up and cancel:** You need to make it easy for people to sign up for and cancel your subscription. If it is too difficult, people will be less likely to do so.
- **Provide excellent customer service:** Your customer service should be flawless for you to retain and attract new subscribers.

By following these tips, you can increase your chances of success in creating a subscription-based model that will make money.

Tips for Successfully Implementing a Subscription-Based Model

To maximize the success of your subscription-based business, consider the following tips:

- **Choose the right niche:** Identify a market segment with a high demand for regular, ongoing access to products or services. Examples of successful markets include software-as-a-service (SaaS), entertainment streaming, and subscription box services for various consumer goods.

- **Create a compelling value proposition:** Communicate the benefits of your subscription offering to potential customers, focusing on convenience, cost savings, and exclusive access to products or services.
- **Offer multiple subscription tiers:** Customers have different subscription options, catering to various budget levels and preferences. This allows you to capture a wider audience and increase customer satisfaction.
- **Focus on customer experience:** Ensure that your subscribers receive exceptional service and support throughout your subscriptions. This includes seamless onboarding, regular communication, and prompt resolution of any issues.
- **Continuously innovate and improve:** Regularly evaluate your subscription offerings and make improvements based on customer feedback and market trends. Doing so will help keep your business competitive and relevant in the long run.

Subscription-based models offer entrepreneurs a powerful strategy for making money and achieving sustainable growth in your businesses.

9. Licensing

Turn your intellectual assets into recurring royalty streams

Licensing allows companies to generate revenue by granting permission to other businesses to use your intellectual property, including trademarks, patents, or technology. In return, the company receives a licensing fee. This revenue stream can be particularly

beneficial for businesses involved in creative, technological, or innovative fields. According to PwC, the global total licensing royalty revenue was worth $280.3 billion in 2018, reflecting the significant potential of this model.

Embracing Licensing as a Profitable Strategy for Entrepreneurs

Licensing allows entrepreneurs to capitalize on your intellectual property (IP) by granting other businesses the right to use your IP in exchange for royalties or fees. According to a report by Statista, the global market value of licensed merchandise reached $292.8 billion in 2019, demonstrating the immense potential of this strategy.

Why Choose Licensing as a Business Strategy?

Licensing offers several advantages over traditional business models, making it an attractive option for entrepreneurs. Some of these benefits include:

- Monetizing intellectual property: Licensing enables entrepreneurs to generate revenue from their IP, such as patents, trademarks, copyrights, and trade secrets, without having to manufacture or distribute products themselves.
- Expanding your market reach: By partnering with established companies, entrepreneurs can leverage the licensee's resources, distribution channels, and customer base to expand their market reach and increase sales.
- Lower risks: Licensing involves lower financial risk compared to launching a new product or entering a new market independently as it requires minimal upfront investment.
- Enhanced brand visibility: Licensing agreements can help increase brand awareness and credibility as licensees often invest in marketing and promoting the licensed products.

Tips for Successfully Implementing a Licensing Strategy

To maximize the success of your licensing strategy, consider the following tips:

- **Protect your intellectual property:** Ensure your IP is properly registered and protected through patents, trademarks, copyrights, or trade secrets before entering into licensing agreements.
- **Identify potential licensees:** Research potential licensees to identify companies that align with your brand values, have strong distribution channels, and possess the necessary resources to successfully market and sell your licensed products.
- **Negotiate favorable terms:** When negotiating licensing agreements, focus on securing favorable terms that protect your interests, such as royalties, minimum guarantees, and performance clauses.
- **Monitor licensee performance:** Actively monitor the performance of your licensees to ensure they are meeting your contractual obligations, maintaining the quality of your brand, and yielding the expected revenue.
- **Explore new opportunities:** Continuously evaluate market trends and potential licensing opportunities to expand your portfolio and generate additional revenue streams.

The Power of Licensing for Sustainable Business Growth

By carefully protecting their intellectual property, selecting the right licensees, and actively managing their licensing partnerships, entrepreneurs can build a successful licensing business.

10. Merchandising

Monetize your brand identity through physical merchandise

For companies with strong brand recognition or influence, selling merchandise can serve as a substantial revenue stream. This could range from t-shirts and mugs to customized accessories. A Statista report predicts the global licensed merchandise market will reach $425 billion by 2028, emphasizing the potential this area holds.

Embracing Merchandising as a Profitable Strategy for Entrepreneurs

Merchandising involves creating and selling branded products to promote a company or brand. According to a report by Grand View Research, the global licensed merchandise market size was valued at $280.3 billion in 2019 and is expected to grow at a compound annual growth rate (CAGR) of 4.1% through 2027.

Why Choose Merchandising as a Business Strategy?

Merchandising offers several advantages over traditional business models, making it an attractive option for entrepreneurs. Some of these benefits include:

- Increased brand awareness: Merchandising helps increase your brand's visibility and recognition, as customers who purchase and use your branded products become walking advertisements.
- Customer loyalty: Branded merchandise can foster a sense of belonging and loyalty among customers, encouraging them to continue supporting your business and recommending it to others.

- Additional revenue stream: Selling branded merchandise provides an additional revenue stream that can supplement your core business offerings and contribute to overall profitability.
- Low entry barriers: Merchandising typically requires a minimal upfront investment, making it a viable option for entrepreneurs looking to test the market or expand their product offerings.

Tips for Successfully Implementing a Merchandising Strategy

To maximize the success of your merchandising strategy, consider the following tips:

- **Identify your target audience:** Understand your target customer base and create merchandise that appeals to your preferences and interests while remaining true to your brand identity.
- **Choose high-quality products:** Ensure the merchandise you offer is of high quality and reflects positively on your brand. This may involve partnering with reputable suppliers and manufacturers.
- **Create eye-catching designs:** Invest in producing visually appealing and memorable designs that showcase your brand's personality and values, making your merchandise stand out from the competition.
- **Leverage multiple sales channels:** Utilize both online and offline sales channels to reach your target audience, including e-commerce platforms, social media, and physical retail locations.
- **Promote your merchandise:** Actively promote your branded merchandise through targeted marketing campaigns, special offers, and collaborations with influencers or partners.

By carefully identifying their target audience, offering high-quality products, and leveraging multiple sales channels, entrepreneurs can build a successful merchandising business.

11. Crowdfunding

Validate and fund your concept with early supporter contributions

Crowdfunding entails raising small amounts of money from a large number of people, typically through an online crowdfunding platform. This model can be an excellent way for startups or small businesses to raise capital. The funds, depending on the crowdfunding model used, can be treated as donations, investments, or pre-orders for a product. The global crowdfunding market size was valued at $13.93 billion in 2019 and is expected to reach $28.77 billion by 2025, according to Mordor Intelligence.

Embracing Crowdfunding as a Profitable Strategy for Entrepreneurs

According to a report by Statista, the global crowdfunding market is expected to grow at a CAGR of 16% between 2020 and 2025.

Why Choose Crowdfunding as a Business Strategy?

Crowdfunding offers several advantages over traditional fundraising methods, making it an attractive option for entrepreneurs. Some of these benefits include:

- **Access to capital:** Crowdfunding provides entrepreneurs with an alternative source of funding, which can be particularly valuable for startups and small businesses that may struggle to secure financing through traditional channels.
- **Market validation:** By gauging the interest and support of potential customers through crowdfunding

campaigns, entrepreneurs can validate their ideas and products before investing significant time and resources into development.

- **Increased visibility:** Successful crowdfunding campaigns can help raise awareness and generate buzz around a project or venture, potentially attracting additional investors, partners, and customers.
- **Community engagement:** Crowdfunding allows entrepreneurs to engage with their target audience and build a community of supporters who are invested in the success of their project or venture.

Tips for Successfully Implementing a Crowdfunding Strategy

To maximize the success of your crowdfunding campaign, consider the following tips:

- **Choose the right platform:** Select a crowdfunding outlet that aligns with your project's goals, target audience, and funding requirements. Popular platforms include Kickstarter, Indiegogo, and GoFundMe, among others.
- **Craft an engaging story:** To captivate potential backers for your crowdfunding project, it's crucial to articulate a compelling narrative. This narrative should effectively communicate your passion, vision, and the distinctive aspects of your project that set it apart.

For instance, if you're raising funds to launch a sustainable fashion brand, your narrative might detail your passion for environmental preservation, the need for sustainable alternatives in the fashion industry, and the unique eco-friendly materials and ethical manufacturing processes your brand employs. This story not only illustrates the purpose of your project but also connects emotionally with potential backers who share similar values, inspiring them to contribute to your cause.

- **Set realistic funding goals:** Establish a clear and achievable funding goal that covers the costs of your project or venture while also accounting for any fees associated with the crowdfunding platform and payment processing.
- **Offer enticing rewards:** Provide attractive rewards or incentives to encourage backers to support your campaign. These can include early access to products, exclusive experiences, or personalized items.
- **Promote your campaign:** Actively promote your crowdfunding campaign through social media, email marketing, public relations, and other marketing channels to reach your target audience and generate interest in your project or venture.

By carefully selecting the right platform, crafting a compelling story, and actively promoting their campaigns, entrepreneurs can raise funds to bring their projects or ventures to life.

———

Halfway There...
A Quick Note from S.R. Brown

WRITING How to Make Money in Business Online has been all about giving you the playbook to crush it online. My goal? To hand you the tools, strategies, and mindset shifts that actually work—not fluff. If this book has sparked new ideas, pushed you to take action, or made you think bigger, I want to hear about it.

Can you take a moment to help another entrepreneur? Scan the QR code below to leave a review on Amazon. Your feedback means the world to me—and it inspires others to take action and start winning.

Let's dominate,
S.R. Brown

12. Other Ideas To Make Money

- **Dropshipping:** This low-risk, low-investment online business model involves selling products from third-party suppliers directly shipping to your customers. Ideal for those venturing into the eCommerce realm.
- **Blogging:** Create content on a specific topic and generate revenue through advertising, sponsored posts, or selling your products and services.
- **Bookkeeping:** Offer your services to businesses and charge them on an hourly basis, monthly retainer, or per-service basis, creating a steady stream of income. According to ZipRecruiter, as of 2023, the average annual pay for an online bookkeeper in the United States is $58,525, indicating the potential for profitability in this field.
- **Freelancing:** A versatile online business model where you offer your skills and expertise in writing, graphic design, web development, or social media management. Capitalizing on your unique skills allows you to establish a successful online business, work on your own terms, and achieve financial freedom.

Evaluating and Choosing Business Models to Make Money in Business

Choosing a suitable business model is a critical step every entrepreneur must take. Your business model is essentially the framework that outlines how your venture will capture value, in other words, how it will generate revenue. Let's evaluate and choose the suitable business model for your venture.

Business Model Types:

At its core, a business model describes how your company creates, delivers, and captures value. It answers pivotal questions about who your customers are, what they value, and how you'll make money by providing that value. While there are many types of business models, they generally fall into these broad categories:

1. **Product-based:** This framework involves selling physical goods directly to consumers, such as a retail clothing store.
2. **Service-based:** In this model, you're selling a skill or a type of expertise. Examples include consulting firms, hair salons, and auto repair shops.
3. **Subscription-based:** This format charges customers a recurring fee—usually monthly or yearly—to access a product or service. Examples include Netflix or software-as-a-service (SaaS) companies like Salesforce.
4. **Freemium:** In this model, basic features of a product or service are provided free of charge, but users are charged for premium features and functionalities. LinkedIn uses this business model.
5. **Commission-based:** In this model, a business takes a percentage of the transaction value between two parties. For instance, Airbnb takes a commission for every booking made through its platform.

6. **E-commerce:** This refers to selling products or services online. The products could be physical (books, clothing, hardware) or digital (e-books, downloadable music, software, apps).

Evaluating Business Models:

Now that you understand the different types of business models, the next step is to evaluate them. Here's what to consider:

1. **Customer Demand:** Understanding your target market is key. What do your potential customers want, and how much will they pay?
2. **Revenue Generation:** How quickly and reliably can this model generate revenue? Some models may have a faster return on investment than others.
3. **Scalability:** Can the business model scale as your business grows? A model that works for a small-scale operation might not be as efficient once the business expands.
4. **Risk:** Every business model comes with its risks. Understanding these risks and assessing whether they are acceptable and manageable for your particular situation is crucial.
5. **Profit Margins:** Different business models can also have vastly different profit margins. Consider the costs associated with your model of choice and whether it can yield profitable returns.

Choosing a Business Model:

The choice of business model is highly dependent on your specific circumstances, market, and the nature of the product or service you are offering. Your business model should align with your business goals, target customer behaviors, and market dynamics.

It's also important to remember that choosing a business model isn't a one-time decision. As your business grows and market dynamics change, it might need to evolve. Some companies may even use a combination of different models.

Re-Evaluating and Choosing Business Models to Accelerate Business Growth for Experienced Entrepreneurs

Even for experienced entrepreneurs, continuously evaluating and updating business models is essential to stay competitive and relevant in a rapidly evolving marketplace. The business model that worked when you first launched your business might need adjustments to align with shifts in customer preferences, technological advancements, and competitive landscapes.

HERE'S how to evaluate and choose business models to spur growth and profit in a more advanced stage of your business.

1. Survey Your Landscape:

As an experienced entrepreneur, you have likely built a strong understanding of your industry and competitors. Use this knowledge to identify successful business models within your niche and analyze what makes them effective. It's also beneficial to look beyond your industry to discover innovative frameworks that could apply to your business.

2. Leverage Data:

One advantage you have as an established entrepreneur is access to historical and real-time data. Use this to assess the profitability and viability of your current model. Look at key performance indicators, such as revenue, profit margin, customer retention, and acquisition costs. With these metrics, you can gauge whether your current model still drives your business toward your goals or if adjustments are needed.

3. Embrace Flexibility:

In the startup phase, a particular business model might have worked because it was simple and easy to implement. However, as your business grows and matures, embracing more complex models to maximize your revenue may be necessary. This could include incorporating multiple revenue streams, such as a combination of product sales, services, and subscription fees.

4. Innovation and Experimentation:

Innovation is key in a rapidly evolving business environment. Don't shy away from experimenting with new business models. Consider testing new models on a small scale, measure your effectiveness, and adjust accordingly. Even if an experiment doesn't pan out, the insights gained can help inform future decisions.

5. Customer-Centric Approach:

As the marketplace evolves, so do your customers' needs and preferences. Regularly surveying your customers or conducting market research can provide insights into your changing behaviors. Align your business model to these changing customer needs. For instance, if your customers increasingly prefer digital services, pivoting towards e-commerce or a SaaS model might be a lucrative move.

6. Sustainability and Long-Term Growth:

While some business models may provide quick financial gains, they may not be sustainable in the long run. Consider whether the business model aligns with your vision for the company's future and can drive long-term growth. Also, assess the model's impact on the environment and society, as sustainable and ethical business practices are becoming increasingly important to consumers.

As an experienced entrepreneur, re-evaluating and refining your business model is a powerful strategy to stay competitive and drive growth. Leveraging industry insights, customer data, and a willingness to innovate and experiment can lead to finding a business model that propels your business toward greater success.

Here's a table outlining key differences between new and experienced entrepreneurs when evaluating and choosing business models to make money in business:

Aspect	New Entrepreneurs	Experienced Entrepreneurs
Understanding of Business Models	May have a basic understanding of different business models, often from theory or limited practice.	Typically have a deeper understanding of various business models from their past experiences.
Risk Tolerance	Might prefer safer, more straightforward models as they're still learning and may not have as much capital to risk.	Likely to have a higher tolerance for risk, which may allow them to experiment with innovative or complex business models.
Use of Data	Limited historical data. Decisions may rely more on market research and projections.	Have access to historical and real-time data from their existing businesses to inform their decisions.
Flexibility	More likely to stick with the initial business model due to a lack of resources or experience to pivot or adapt to market needs.	More likely to adapt and change their business model in response to market changes and growth opportunities.
Customer Understanding	May still be identifying their target market and understanding customer preferences.	Have a solid understanding of their customer base and are able to align their business strategies to fit customer needs.
Long-Term Perspective	May focus more on short-term viability and immediate profitability.	More likely to focus on long-term sustainability and growth when making business decisions.
Approach to Innovation	May follow more traditional or existing models in their industry.	More open to experimentation and innovation in business models due to experience and established success.

Table 1: Differences between new and experienced entrepreneurs when evaluating and choosing business models to make money in business

Setting Benchmarks and Identifying Money-Making Opportunities

Establishing benchmarks and pinpointing money-making opportunities is a smart strategy that can really ignite your business's growth. These steps offer a gauge for success and help steer your company towards those lucrative areas worth concentrating on.

Before we jump into the nitty-gritty of setting benchmarks and discovering opportunities, let's take a moment to clarify what benchmarks actually mean.

What are benchmarks?

Benchmarks are standards or points of reference used to measure performance. In business, benchmarks are often employed to compare the performance of different companies or products. They can also be used to track a company's performance over time.

Using Benchmarks To Measure Performance and Make Money

Benchmarks provide entrepreneurs with a standard against which they can measure their own business's performance. They offer valuable insights into industry standards and successful practices. Here's a specific example of how an entrepreneur might use benchmarks to improve their business and profitability:

Suppose you're running an eCommerce store selling handmade jewelry. You're doing well, but you feel there's room for improvement, particularly in your website's conversion rate. You decide to use benchmarking to help improve this key performance indicator (KPI).

First, you conduct research and find out that the average conversion rate for eCommerce stores in your industry is 2.5%. Upon reviewing your own metrics, you discover that your site's conversion rate is currently at 1.5%. Now, you have a clear benchmark to aim for - you know that other businesses in your sector are achieving a higher conversion rate, so it's feasible for you to reach that, too.

Using this benchmark, you can now devise strategies to improve your conversion rate. This might involve tweaking your website design for a better user experience, improving your product descriptions, or offering competitive pricing.

By constantly monitoring your performance against the benchmark, you'll be able to measure the success of your efforts and adjust your strategies accordingly. This way, benchmarks can guide you towards improved performance, higher conversion rates, and ultimately, increased profitability.

Benchmark Types:

There are many different types of benchmarks, but some of the most common include:

- **Financial benchmarks:** These benchmarks measure the financial performance of a company, such as its revenue, profit, and return on investment.

- **Operational benchmarks:** These benchmarks measure the efficiency of a company's operations, such as its production output, customer satisfaction, and employee turnover.
- **Competitive benchmarks:** These benchmarks compare a company's performance to its competitors. Benchmarks can be used for a variety of purposes, including:
- **To set goals:** Benchmarks can be used to set goals for a company's performance. For example, a company might set a goal of increasing its revenue by 10% in the next year.
- **To track progress:** Benchmarks can also be utilized to track a company's progress over time. For example, a

company might track its revenue growth each quarter to see if it is on track to meet its goals.

- **To identify areas for improvement:** You can also use benchmarks to identify areas where a company can improve its performance. For example, if a company's customer satisfaction is below average, it might need to improve its customer service.

Benchmarks can be a valuable tool for businesses of all sizes. By using benchmarks, companies can improve their performance, identify improvement areas, and set future goals.

Here are some examples of how businesses use benchmarks:

- A company might use financial benchmarks to compare its revenue to the revenue of its competitors. This information could help the company set more realistic goals for its own revenue growth.

- A company might use operational benchmarks to track its production output over time. This information could help the company identify areas where it can improve its efficiency.

- A company might use competitive benchmarks to compare its customer satisfaction to that of its competitors. This information could help the company improve its customer service.

By using benchmarks, businesses can gain valuable insights into their performance and make informed decisions about how to improve.

Here's how you can effectively approach these steps:

Setting Benchmarks

1. Understand your business inside and out: Begin with a thorough understanding of your business. This

encompasses your financials, operations, sales, and marketing efforts and your competitive environment. Understanding these elements will guide you in setting meaningful and achievable benchmarks.

2. Identify Key Performance Indicators (KPIs): These metrics should align with your business goals. If your primary goal is to increase revenue, your KPIs might include sales growth rate, monthly recurring revenue, or customer lifetime value. If your focus is improving operational efficiency, benchmarks might involve reducing production time or decreasing operating costs.

3. Set SMART goals: Benchmarks should be Specific, Measurable, Achievable, Relevant, and Time-bound (SMART). For instance, instead of a vague goal like "increase sales," a SMART goal would be "increase sales by 20% over the next quarter."

4. Monitor and Adjust: Business environments are dynamic. Regularly reviewing your benchmarks and adjusting them as necessary will ensure they remain relevant and continue to drive progress.

Identifying Opportunities to Make Money

1. **Assess your market:** A comprehensive understanding of your market, including trends, customer behaviors, and competitive landscape, can help identify areas of opportunity.

2. **Listen to your customers:** Your customers can be a valuable source of insights. Regular feedback, reviews, and interactions can reveal unmet needs or potential areas for growth.

3. **Leverage data and analytics:** Use data from sales, marketing, and operations to identify patterns, trends, and areas for improvement. Data analytics can provide insights into profitable segments, successful products, and customer behavior.

4. **Diversify revenue streams:** Consider ways you can diversify your revenue. This could involve introducing new products or services, exploring different business models (like subscriptions or memberships), or tapping into new markets.

5. **Innovate continuously:** The businesses that thrive are often those that innovate regularly. Whether it's improving your product or service, refining your processes, or creating a better customer experience, innovation can open up new opportunities for making money.

Setting benchmarks and identifying money-making opportunities are integral parts of business growth strategy. By combining a clear understanding of their business and market, leveraging data, listening to their customers, and fostering a culture of innovation, entrepreneurs can effectively steer their businesses toward greater profitability and success.

Setting Benchmarks and Identifying Opportunities as Experienced Entrepreneurs

Experienced entrepreneurs have the advantage of a deep knowledge base and potentially a wider network to leverage. Here are some insightful strategies for setting benchmarks and identifying business opportunities tailored to seasoned businesspersons:

Setting Benchmarks as Experienced Entrepreneurs

1. **Benchmark against past performance:** As an experienced entrepreneur, you have historical data that you can leverage. Comparing current performances against past performances can be a great way to set benchmarks.

2. **Use industry benchmarks:** Besides setting benchmarks based on your own performance, consider

using industry benchmarks. These can provide a broader context to measure your business's success and can be particularly useful in understanding your standing within your specific industry.

3. **Take into account the maturity of the business:** Your benchmarks should align with the lifecycle stage of your business. For mature businesses, benchmarks might focus on efficiency, cost control, and customer retention rather than the aggressive growth targets that might be suitable for younger companies.

4. **Involve your team:** Ensure your team is involved in the benchmarking process. This will not only encourage your buy-in but also provide you with diverse perspectives that can lead to more balanced and realistic benchmarks.

Identifying Opportunities to Make Money as Experienced Entrepreneurs

1. **Leverage existing customer base:** One of the most cost- effective ways to increase revenue is to sell more to your existing customers. Consider opportunities for upselling, cross-selling, or introducing loyalty programs.

2. **Strategic partnerships:** As an experienced entrepreneur, you likely have a large network. Consider opportunities for strategic partnerships that could open up new revenue streams.

3. **Look at adjacent markets:** Having established a successful business model, you can examine adjacent markets where your product or service may be valuable. This could involve expanding into new geographic regions or targeting a new demographic within your existing market.

4. **Re-evaluate business model:** It might be time to re-evaluate your business model to unlock new opportunities. Could a subscription model add a stable

revenue stream? Would offering a premium service attract a new segment of clients?

5. **Innovation:** Despite your success, don't rest on your laurels. Continue to innovate - whether that's in your product line, your processes, or your service offerings. New products, particularly, can be a great way to boost interest and revenue.

In sum, experienced entrepreneurs can use their existing data, customer base, and networks to identify new opportunities and set more accurate and contextual benchmarks. The key is to stay flexible, keep innovating, and always be open to the idea of reinvention when necessary.

Here's a table outlining key differences between new and experienced entrepreneurs when setting benchmarks and identifying opportunities:

Aspect	New Entrepreneurs	Experienced Entrepreneurs
Setting Benchmarks	Tend to rely on industry norms, competitive analysis, and future projections due to a lack of historical business data.	Typically, leverage historical data and past performance in setting more precise, company-specific benchmarks.
Risk Tolerance for Benchmarks	May set more conservative benchmarks as they navigate their business's initial stages.	Likely to set more ambitious benchmarks, based on knowledge, experience, and resources.
Source of Opportunities	Opportunities often stem from new market trends, unmet customer needs, and innovative ideas.	Opportunities often from existing customers, established networks, strategic partnerships, and expansion into adjacent markets.
Approach to Innovation	Innovation often revolves around the product or service as they strive to establish a market presence.	Innovation can be more strategic and multifaceted, encompassing products, services, processes, and business models.
Use of Data for Opportunities	Limited data may constrain their ability to identify opportunities. They often rely on market research and customer feedback.	Have access to a wealth of data from their own business operations, which helps them pinpoint opportunities for growth and expansion.
Approach to New Revenue Streams	May focus on establishing a core revenue stream before diversifying.	More likely to explore and integrate multiple revenue streams, leveraging their understanding of the market and customer base.

Table 2: Key differences between new and experienced entrepreneurs when setting benchmarks and identifying opportunities

CHAPTER 4

Defining Your Business Identity

Determine the relationship between pinpointing your ideal customer; the person you genuinely want to serve, and your business identity, especially when you're just starting out and might not have a clear idea of what your brand is.

Why Business Identity Matters

Your business identity is the core of what your company stands for. It reflects your values, mission, and the special offerings that set you apart. Identifying your ideal customer is a key aspect of creating this identity because it helps you understand who you're trying to serve and what problems you're aiming to solve for them.

When you clearly understand your ideal customer, you can tailor every aspect of your business – from messaging and marketing to product development and customer service – to meet your specific needs and preferences. This targeted approach ensures that your business identity is consistent, cohesive, and well-aligned with the audience you want to serve.

Business Identity Alignment

Aligning your business identity with your ideal customer involves several essential steps:

- **Customer profile:** Create a detailed profile of your ideal customer, including demographics, interests, pain points, and goals. This will help you understand your needs and preferences, allowing you to develop products, services, and messaging that resonate with them.

- **Clear message:** Develop a clear and compelling message that communicates the benefits of your offerings and why customers should choose you over competitors. Make sure this message speaks directly to your ideal customer and highlights the unique advantages they'll receive from your products or services.
- **Consistent message:** Craft messaging and marketing materials that consistently reflect your business identity and speak to your ideal customer's needs, desires, and pain points. This will help reinforce your image and foster trust with your target audience.
- **Product and service development:** Design and refine your products and services to specifically address the needs, preferences, and challenges of your ideal customer. This will strengthen your business identity by demonstrating your commitment to meeting the unique needs of your target audience.

By aligning your business identity with your ideal customer, you'll create a powerful and cohesive image that resonates with your audience, ultimately leading to stronger customer relationships, increased loyalty, and long-term success.

Defining Your Business Identity as Experienced Entrepreneurs

Alright, let's weave these concepts together with clear steps to shape your business identity:

Have a Bold Vision:

Dream big about your future. Visualize your business reaching far, deep, and wide. Think about serving thousands, if not millions.

Hold onto this dream, as it will be instrumental in helping you make decisions.

How does this help you make money in business?

A bold vision can help you define your business identity, set ambitious goals, stand out from the competition, and build a strong brand. All of these things can lead to increased profitability and success. According to a study by the Harvard Business Review, businesses with a bold vision are 21% more likely to exceed their revenue goals.

A bold vision gives you something to strive for and helps you stay motivated when things get tough. When you have a bold vision, you are more likely to take risks and make decisions that will help you achieve your goals.

By dreaming big, setting specific yet realistic goals, and sharing your vision with others, you create a clear roadmap toward achieving your objectives. This strong sense of direction keeps you motivated during challenging times and encourages risk-taking, ultimately leading to business growth and increased revenue.

Here are some tips for creating a bold vision for your business: Think big. What do you really want to achieve with your business? How many people do you want to serve? How much impact do you want to have?

- **Be specific.** Your vision should be specific enough that you can measure your progress. What are your specific goals for revenue, customer growth, and market share?
- **Be realistic.** Your vision should be realistic but challenging. If it is too easy, you won't be motivated to achieve it. But if it is too difficult, you may get discouraged and give up.
- **Write it down.** Once you have a clear vision for your business, write it down. This will help you stay focused and motivated.

- **Share it with others.** Share your vision with your team, customers, and investors. This will help you get the support you need to achieve your goals.

A bold vision is essential for any entrepreneur. It will help you achieve your goals. So, dream big, be specific, be realistic, write it down, and share it with others.

Here are some examples of bold visions from successful entrepreneurs not named Bezos, Zuckerberg, or Musk:

- Whitney Wolfe Herd: Whitney Wolfe Herd is the founder and CEO of Bumble, a popular dating app that empowers women by allowing them to make the first move. She co-founded Tinder, another well-known dating app, but left the company and went on to establish Bumble in 2014. Bumble quickly gained popularity and became a significant competitor in the online dating industry. In 2021, she made her company public, becoming the youngest female CEO ever to take a U.S. company public.

- Jewel Burks Solomon: Jewel Burks Solomon co-founded Partpic, a visual recognition technology company. Partpic developed an innovative solution that uses artificial intelligence to identify and locate replacement parts for industrial equipment by analyzing images. In 2016, the company was acquired by Amazon.

- Brian Chesky: Brian Chesky is the co-founder and CEO of Airbnb, the famous online marketplace for vacation rentals and experiences. Chesky and his co-founders launched the platform in 2008 to connect travelers with unique accommodation options.

These are just a few examples of bold visions that have helped entrepreneurs achieve great things. If you have a bold vision for your business, don't be afraid to share it with the world. It could be the key to your success.

How Does Crafting Your Bold Vision Make You Money In Business?

- A Harvard Business Review study found that businesses with a bold vision were more likely to have a clear understanding of their target market, a strong value proposition, and a well- defined plan for growth. These businesses were also more likely to have a strong leadership team and a culture that encourages innovation and risk-taking.

The study's findings suggest that having a bold vision can be a critical factor in a business's success. If you are starting a business or looking to grow your existing business, having a clear and ambitious vision for what you want to achieve is important. Having a bold vision can help you attract and retain top talent, exceed your revenue goals, and grow your market share.

- The Temkin Group study found that businesses with a bold vision were 17% more likely to grow their market share than businesses without a bold vision.
- A study by the Korn Ferry Institute found that businesses with a bold vision were more likely to attract and retain top talent than businesses without a bold vision.

The studies cited above provide evidence that having a bold vision can help businesses achieve financial success. Businesses that dare take risks are more likely to attract and retain top talent, which can lead to increased productivity and innovation.

Here are some tips for creating a bold vision for your business:

- Start by defining your target market. Who are you trying

to reach with your business? What are your needs and wants?

- What problem are you trying to solve? What pain points is your target market experiencing?
- What makes your business unique? What can you offer your target market that no one else can?
- What are your goals? What do you want to achieve with your business?
- How will you measure your success? How will you know if you have achieved your goals? Once you have a clear vision for your business, you can start to develop a plan to achieve it. This plan should include strategies for marketing, sales, and operations.

It is important to remember that your vision will not be achieved overnight. It will take time, hard work, and dedication. However, you are more likely to succeed if you are thorough and organized.

2. Craft Your Unique Story:

Like every superhero, your business needs an origin story. What motivated you to start? How are you changing the world one customer at a time? Your narrative sets you apart, and it's the heartbeat of your brand. You should be communicating that story as part of your business identity.

How does this help you make money in business?

Having a strong brand story can help businesses achieve financial success. Studies have found that businesses with a strong brand story can command a price premium of up to 20%, grow your revenue 20% faster than your competitors, and are 70% more likely to be chosen by consumers.

Here are some tips for crafting a unique story for your business:

- **Be personal.** Your story should be personal and relatable. Share your experiences, motivations, and goals. Let your customers get to know you on a personal level.

- **Be specific.** Don't just tell your customers that you're passionate about your business. Tell them why you're passionate. What problem are you trying to solve? How is your business making a difference in the world?
- **Be authentic.** Don't try to be someone you're not. Be yourself and let your personality shine through in your story. Your customers will appreciate your authenticity.
- **Be consistent.** Once you've crafted your story, share it consistently across all your marketing channels. This will help you build a strong brand identity and create a connection with your customers.

Businesses should craft a strong brand story that is relevant to their target audience, is kept concise, utilizes storytelling techniques, and maintains authenticity.

Following these tips, you can craft a unique story for your business to help you connect with your customers and build a strong brand identity.

Here are some examples of businesses that have successfully crafted unique stories:

- **Warby Parker:** An online eyewear retailer that sells high- quality glasses at a fraction of the price of traditional eyewear retailers. The company's story is one of innovation and disruption. Warby Parker was founded on the belief that everyone should access affordable, high-quality eyewear. The company has disrupted the traditional eyewear industry by selling glasses directly to consumers online.
- **TOMS:** A shoe company that donates one pair of shoes for every pair sold. The company's story is one of giving back. TOMS was founded on the belief that for every pair of shoes sold, a new pair would be given to a child in need. The company has donated over 80 million pairs of shoes to needy children in over 90 countries.

- **Airbnb:** A home-sharing company founded on the belief that people can connect meaningfully by sharing your homes. The company's story is one of community and connection. It has created a community of over 4 million hosts and guests who have shared over 1 billion nights.

These are just a few examples of businesses that have successfully crafted unique stories and have connected with their customers and built strong brand identities by sharing them.

If you want to succeed in business, crafting a unique story for your business is important. Your story will help you connect with your customers, build a strong brand identity, and achieve your goals.

How Does Crafting Your Unique Story Make You Money In Business?

As previously mentioned, businesses that can craft a unique story that resonates with their customers are more likely to be successful.

- Unique stories help businesses stand out from the competition. In today's crowded marketplace, it's more important than ever for companies to have a unique narrative that sets them apart from the competition. Indeed, when customers can connect with a business on a personal level, they're more likely to become loyal customers.
- Unique stories help businesses build trust with customers. When customers know the story behind a business, they're more likely to trust that business. This trust can lead to increased sales and revenue.
- Unique stories help businesses create a positive brand image. A positive brand image can help businesses attract and retain new customers. When customers

positively perceive a business, they're more likely to do business with that business again in the future.

There is a clear financial benefit to having a strong brand story.

- A study by the National Retail Federation found that 70% of consumers are likelier to shop with a retailer with a strong brand story.
- A study by the McKinsey & Company found that companies with strong brands can command a price premium of up to 20%.
- A study by the Boston Consulting Group found that companies with strong brands can grow their revenue 20% faster than their competitors.

Here are some additional tips for crafting a unique story for your business:

- **Make it relevant to your target audience.** Your story should be relevant to the people you're trying to reach. What are your needs and wants? What are your pain points? How can your business help them?
- **Keep it short and sweet.** People have short attention spans, so keep your story short and to the point. Get to the heart of your message quickly and effectively.
- **Use storytelling techniques.** Storytelling is a powerful way to connect with people on an emotional level. Use storytelling techniques like plot, character development, and conflict to make your story engaging and memorable.
- **Be authentic.** People can spot a fake from a mile away. Be authentic and genuine in your story. Let your personality shine through.

By following these tips, you can craft a unique story for your business that will help you connect with your customers, build a strong brand identity, and achieve your goals.

3. Keep Your Eyes on the Horizon:

Beware of the immediate issues, challenges, or trends that could potentially distract you or lead you to make decisions that do not align with your long-term vision.

As an entrepreneur, you'll face numerous challenges and distractions that may tempt you to make short-term focused decisions. Despite these pressures, it's crucial to remain steadfast and make choices that are aligned with your envisioned future for your business.

How does this help you make money in business?

According to a Harvard Business Review study, companies with a clear vision are 23% more likely to surpass revenue targets. Focusing on long-term goals leads to greater success, and businesses with a distinct vision, robust brand, and high customer satisfaction tend to be more profitable.

What does keeping your eyes on the horizon mean to build a strong business identity?

Each decision you make significantly contributes to your brand's overall development and identity. So, every choice should be evaluated with its potential long-term impact in mind.

Will the decision help you achieve your goals? Will it make your business more competitive? Will it improve your customer experience? If the answer is no, then it is probably not a good decision.

There will be times when things get tough, and you may feel like giving up. But it is important to remember that these tough times are temporary. If you stay focused on your long-term goals and make decisions that align with your future vision, you will eventually reach your destination.

The choices you make today will shape the future of your business. Every decision you make, big or small, is a brick in the castle of your brand. Ensure you build a strong brand that will stand the test of time.

How does keeping your eyes on the horizon make you money in business?

Here is a summary of how the following help define your business identity and lead to making money:

- Keep your eyes on the horizon. This means making decisions that align with your long-term goals, even during challenging times. Focusing on the future and ensuring each choice contributes to building a strong brand creates a solid foundation for your business identity. This strategic approach leads to increased competitiveness, improved customer experience, and greater financial success.
- Remember, every choice you make, big or small, is a brick in the castle of your brand. The choices you make today will shape the future of your business. Ensure you build a strong brand that will stand the test of time.

Here are some facts and figures:

- A study by Harvard Business Review found that companies with a clear vision are 23% more likely to exceed your revenue goals.
- A study by Bain & Company found that companies with strong brands are 10% more likely to be profitable.
- A study by the Temkin Group found that companies with a high customer satisfaction score are five times more likely to be profitable.

These studies suggest there is a clear link between having a clear vision, a strong brand, and profitability. Companies that can keep their eyes on the horizon and make decisions that align with their long-term goals are more likely to be successful.

It is important to note that these are just averages. The actual results will vary depending on a number of factors, such as the industry, the size of the company, and the quality of the decisions made. However, the studies cited above suggest that there is a clear financial benefit to keeping your eyes on the horizon and making decisions that align with your long-term goals.

4. Shape Your Playground:

Your business is your sandbox, and you're the sculptor. Create a work environment that fuels creativity and encourages teamwork. Think about the kind of culture that aligns with your brand's values and ethos.

How does this help you make money in business?

A workspace with great culture can boost employee productivity by 21%, reduce turnover rates by 30%, and increase customer satisfaction by 12%, ultimately raising profits by as much as $7,000 per employee annually. By creating a positive and engaging work environment, businesses can improve their bottom line in a number of ways, from saving on employee recruiting and training costs to increased loyalty and customer satisfaction, which leads to increased sales.

Creating the ideal work environment and culture is vital to defining your business identity and directly contributing to your business's profitability. Let's break down how this works.

Fostering Creativity:

Creativity is the lifeblood of innovation, and innovation drives business growth. When you build an environment that encourages creativity, you foster a breeding ground for new ideas. This could result in developing unique products, services, or solutions that set you apart from the competition, leading to increased customer interest and sales.

Encouraging Teamwork:

A culture that encourages teamwork promotes sharing ideas and knowledge, resulting in improved problem-solving, more efficient work processes, and better products or services. These efficiencies can reduce costs and increase customer satisfaction, both of which can boost your bottom line.

Reflecting Your Brand's Values and Ethos:

An authentic and positive company culture can be a powerful brand asset. When your work environment reflects your brand's values, it not only helps attract and retain the right talent but also sends a strong message to customers about what your brand stands for. Customers are more likely to support companies whose values align with your own, which can result in increased customer loyalty and sales.

Attracting Talent:

Finally, a positive and engaging work environment can help attract top talent. Having a team of skilled and motivated employees is crucial to business success. Employees who feel valued and inspired in your workspace are more likely to produce high-quality work, leading to increased productivity and profitability.

How you shape your "playground" or work environment can significantly impact your business identity and profitability. By fostering a culture of creativity and teamwork that reflects

your brand's values, you can boost innovation, efficiency, customer loyalty, and employee satisfaction, all of which contribute to business success.

Here are two examples of how businesses have benefited from shaping your playground:

- Zappos is known for its strong company culture. The business has a casual dress code, unlimited vacation days, and a focus on employee happiness. As a result of its strong company culture, Zappos has been named one of the best places to work in America for several years in a row.
- Google is another company known for its strong company culture. The tech giant offers a variety of perks to its employees, including free food, on-site gyms, and laundry services. Google's strong company culture has helped the business attract top talent and become one of the most successful companies in the world.

By shaping their playground, businesses can create a positive and engaging work environment that will benefit their bottom line.

How does shaping your playground make you money in business?

A positive and engaging work environment can help attract top talent, foster creativity, and teamwork, and boost innovation, efficiency, customer loyalty, and employee satisfaction.

- **Attract top talent:** A study by Glassdoor found that 72% of job seekers consider company culture when deciding where to apply. Another study by LinkedIn found that employees who are happy with their company culture are 21% more likely to stay with their employer for at least five years.
- **Foster creativity:** A study by the Harvard Business Review found that companies with a strong company culture are more likely to be innovative. Another study by the World Economic Forum found that creativity is

one of the top skills employers are looking for in new hires.

- **Boost efficiency:** A study by the Society for Human Resource Management found that companies with a strong culture are likelier to have high employee engagement. Employee engagement is a crucial driver of productivity, and companies with high employee engagement are 21% more profitable than companies with low employee engagement.
- **Increase customer loyalty:** A study by Salesforce found that customers are more likely to do business with companies with a strong company culture. Another study by the Harvard Business Review found that companies with a strong company culture are more likely to have repeat customers.
- **Improve employee satisfaction:** A study by Gallup found that employees who are happy with their company culture are more likely to be engaged in their work. Employee engagement is a crucial driver of job satisfaction; companies with high employee satisfaction have lower turnover rates.

By creating a positive and engaging work environment, businesses can attract top talent, foster creativity and teamwork, and boost innovation, efficiency, customer loyalty, and employee satisfaction. All of these factors contribute to business success.

How does shaping your playground make more money in business?

A positive and engaging work environment can lead to a 21% increase in employee productivity, a 30% decrease in turnover rates, and a 12% increase in customer satisfaction, leading to an increase in profits of up to $7,000 per employee per year.

- A Society for Human Resource Management study found that companies with a positive work environment have 21% more productive employees.
- A study by the Harvard Business Review found that companies with low turnover rates are 30% more profitable than companies with high turnover rates.
- A study by the University of Pennsylvania found that companies with a positive work environment have 12% more satisfied customers.
- A study by Bain & Company found that companies with a customer satisfaction score of 8 or higher are five times more likely to be profitable than companies with a customer satisfaction score of 7 or lower.
- A study by the Temkin Group found that companies with a customer satisfaction score of 9 or higher have a customer retention rate of 96% in comparison, companies with a customer satisfaction score of 6 or lower have a customer retention rate of 85%.
- A study by the American Express Customer Satisfaction Index found that companies with a customer satisfaction score of 8 or higher have a revenue growth rate of 10%. In comparison, companies with a customer satisfaction score of 6 or lower have a revenue growth rate of 3%.

These studies suggest a strong correlation between customer satisfaction and profitability. Companies that can improve customer satisfaction can expect to see a corresponding increase in profits.

It is important to note that the increase in profits of up to $7,000 per employee per year is just an estimate. The actual profit a company can expect from improving customer satisfaction will vary depending on factors such as the industry, the company's size, and the cost of acquiring new customers.

However, the studies cited above suggest there is a clear financial benefit to improving customer satisfaction. Companies that can create a positive and engaging work environment are more likely to have happy and productive employees, leading to improved customer satisfaction and increased profits.

This table underscores the importance of a positive work environment or "shaping your playground" in enhancing employee productivity, customer satisfaction, and business profitability. Investing in a positive work environment can yield significant financial returns.

Impact Area	Study and Findings	How It Increases Profits
Employee Productivity	Society for Human Resource Management: Companies with a positive work environment have 21% more productive employees.	More productive employees can increase output, leading to more sales and profit.
Employee Turnover	Harvard Business Review: Companies with low turnover rates are 30% more profitable.	Lower turnover rates reduce hiring and training costs and maintain continuity, leading to better performance and profitability.
Customer Satisfaction	University of Pennsylvania: Companies with a positive work environment have 12% more satisfied customers.	More satisfied customers can lead to more repeat business and positive word-of-mouth, increasing sales and profits.
Profitability & Customer Satisfaction Score	Bain & Company: Companies with a customer satisfaction score of 5 or higher are 3 times more likely to be profitable.	High customer satisfaction scores strengthen customer loyalty and lead to increased retention rates.
Customer Retention	Teflon Group: Companies with a higher customer retention rate have an average revenue growth rate 5 times higher.	High customer retention rates mean increased revenue from existing customers and reduced costs for acquiring new ones.
Revenue Growth	American Express Customer Satisfaction Index: Companies with a customer satisfaction score of 8 or above have a revenue growth rate of 10%.	Revenue growth increases overall company profitability by expanding the customer base and leveraging increased sales volume and profits.

TABLE 3: *Importance of a positive work environment or "shaping your playground"*

5. Align Your Actions:

When it comes to your brand, consistency is king. Ensure your business values are reflected in every aspect, from customer service to email newsletters. Make sure your actions tell the same story as your words and goals. If you have a team, ensure they can share the brand story.

How this helps you make money in business:

Studies have shown that customers are more likely to do business with, pay more for, and trust companies that have strong brand identities. Companies with strong brand identities are also more likely to have higher market share and be successful.

By being consistent, authentic, empowering, and listening to your customers, you can create a strong brand identity that can translate into loyal customers who buy more from you and more often.

Here are some tips for aligning your actions:

- **Be clear about your values.** What are the core values that are important to your business? These values should be reflected in everything you do, from marketing materials to customer service interactions.
- **Be consistent in your messaging.** Ensure your values are reflected in all your marketing materials, from your website to your social media posts. This will help create a consistent brand experience for your customers.
- **Be authentic.** Don't try to be something you're not. Be genuine and transparent with your customers. They will appreciate your honesty and authenticity.
- **Empower your team.** Ensure your team understands your values and how they should be reflected in their work. This will help create a consistent brand experience across all departments.
- **Listen to your customers.** Get customer feedback and use it to improve your products and services. This will help ensure your brand meets your customers' needs.

By following these tips, you can align your actions and create a strong brand that your customers will love.

Here are some examples of businesses that have walked their talk:

- **Nike:** Known for its commitment to innovation and performance. The company's values are reflected in its products, marketing campaigns, and customer service.
- **Warby Parker:** Committed to making high-quality eyewear more accessible. The company's values are reflected in its affordable prices, free shipping, and generous return policy.
- **Toms:** Committed to giving back. The company's values are reflected in its One-for-One program, which donates a pair of shoes to a child in need for every pair of shoes sold.

These are just a few examples of businesses whose actions match their words. By being consistent with their values, these businesses have built strong brands that their customers love.

If you want your business to succeed, aligning your actions is important. Consistency with your values can create a strong brand that will resonate with your customers.

How does aligning your actions lead to making money?

Here are some specific examples of how aligning your actions can lead to making money:

- A study by Salesforce found that customers are 60% more likely to do business with a company they trust.
- A study by Nielsen found that 70% of consumers are willing to pay more for products and services from companies they trust.
- A study by Harvard Business Review found that companies with strong brand identities have a 20% higher market share than companies with weak brand identities.

As you can see, there is a clear link between aligning your

actions with your goals and making money. By being consistent, authentic, empowering, and listening to your customers, you can create a strong brand identity that will lead to success.

Invest in Your Brand's Persona:

Building a recognizable brand requires time, energy, and financial resources. This is no different than investing time, talent, and money in your products or services. If you are your company's brand, make sure there is brand consistency.

Let's define persona before getting into tips for investing in your brand's persona.

How this helps you make money in business:

A strong brand identity can help businesses attract new customers, create a sense of loyalty among existing customers, and increase sales and prices. Investing in a strong brand identity can help businesses define themselves and make more money.

What is a persona?

A persona is a fictional character created to represent a specific customer or user type. Entrepreneurs can use personas to understand better their customers' needs and motivations, which can help them create products and services that are more likely to be successful.

Here are some of the ways that entrepreneurs can use personas:

- **Research:** Personas can be used to help entrepreneurs conduct research on their target market. By understanding the persona's needs, motivations, and pain points, entrepreneurs can develop products and services that are more likely to meet those needs.
- **Product development:** Personas can be used to help entrepreneurs develop products and services that are

aligned with the needs of their target market. By understanding what the persona wants and needs, entrepreneurs can create products and services more likely to succeed.

- **Marketing:** Personas can help entrepreneurs create marketing campaigns that are more likely to reach and resonate with their target market. By understanding the persona's interests, values, and pain points, entrepreneurs can create marketing campaigns that are more likely to be successful.

Overall, personas are a valuable tool that can help entrepreneurs understand their customers better and create products and services that are more likely to be successful.

Here are some additional tips for entrepreneurs who are using personas:

- **Make sure your personas are accurate:** Personas should be based on research and data. Don't make the mistake of creating personas based on your assumptions or biases.
- **Keep your personas up-to-date:** Personas should be updated as your target market changes. Make sure to review your personas on a regular basis and make changes as needed.
- **Use personas throughout your business:** Personas can be used throughout your business, from product development to marketing to customer service. By using personas across your business, you can ensure that everything aligns with the needs of your target market.

Here are some tips for investing in your brand's persona:

- **Train your employees on your company's culture.** Your employees are the face of your company, so it's important that they understand your brand's

values and how to represent them in their interactions
with customers.

- **Launch marketing initiatives to spread your
  brand's message.** There are many ways to market
  your brand, including advertising, public relations, and
  social media. Choose the marketing channels that are
  most likely to reach your target audience and create
  relevant and engaging content.
- **Be consistent.** Once you've defined your brand's
  persona, you must be consistent in your marketing
  materials and customer interactions. This will help create
  a strong and memorable brand identity.

By following these tips, you can invest in your brand's persona
and create a strong and recognizable brand that will resonate with
your customers.

Here are two examples of businesses that have successfully
invested in their brand's persona:

- **Apple:** Known for its innovative products, sleek design,
  and commitment to customer service. The company's
  brand persona is reflected in everything it does, from its
  marketing campaigns to its retail stores.
- **Starbucks:** Known for its commitment to quality coffee
  and its welcoming atmosphere. The company's brand
  persona is reflected in its stores, marketing campaigns,
  and products.

These are just a few examples of businesses successfully
investing in their brand's persona. By being consistent with their
brand persona, these businesses have built strong brands that their
customers love.

If you want your business to succeed, investing in your brand's
persona is important. Consistent with your brand persona can
create a strong brand that will resonate with your customers.

How does investing in your brand's persona can translate into more money?

Investing in your brand's persona can help define your business identity and lead to making money:

- A strong brand identity helps customers to understand what your business is about and what it stands for. This can make it more likely that they will choose your business over your competitors.
- A strong brand identity can also help create a sense of loyalty among customers. This can lead to repeat business and positive word-of-mouth marketing.
- A strong brand identity can also help attract new customers. When potential customers see that your business has a strong brand identity, they are more likely to trust you and do business with you.

In terms of making money, a strong brand identity can help:

- **Increase sales.** Customers who know and trust your brand are more likely to buy from you.
- **Increase prices.** Customers are often willing to pay more for products and services from brands that they trust.
- **Reduce marketing costs.** When you have a strong brand identity, you don't need to spend as much on marketing to attract new customers.

Overall, investing in your brand's persona is a smart investment that can help improve your business in many ways.

Here are some additional tips for investing in your brand's persona:

- **Make sure your brand persona is consistent across all of your marketing materials.** This means using the same colors, fonts, and images in all of your marketing materials.

- **Make sure your brand persona is consistent in your customer service interactions.** This means being friendly, helpful, and knowledgeable when interacting with customers.
- **Make sure your brand persona is consistent in your employee interactions.** This means hiring employees who are a good fit for your brand and training them on your brand's values.

By following these tips, you can create a strong and consistent brand persona that will help your business to succeed.

———

Business Identity Wrap-Up

In the end, remember that your business identity isn't just your logo or tagline. It's the perception people hold about your company. And these steps will help you shape that perception and build a brand that resonates and endears.

CHAPTER 5

Find the Low-Hanging Fruit to Make Money

Top Customer Pain Points and The Solutions They're Willing to Pay For

Customers are continuously on the lookout for solutions that can alleviate these issues and make their lives more comfortable. In this section, we'll explore the most frequent pain points customers are willing to pay someone to help them solve, along with relevant facts.

7 Pain Points Customers Are Willing to Pay to Solve

Identifying the pain points your customers experience is crucial for developing products and services that truly resonate with them. Below are seven of the most common pain points customers are willing to pay for solutions, along with supporting facts and figures.

Time: The Race Against the Clock

Time is a valuable resource, and customers want to save as much of it as possible. They seek quick and efficient solutions that enable them to get what they need without wasting precious minutes.

According to a study by McKinsey, 70% of customers cite time-saving as a significant factor affecting their satisfaction with a brand.

The same McKinsey study found that a significant percentage of customer buying experiences are based on how the customer feels they are being treated, particularly in terms of their time.

Customers appreciate businesses that respect their time and offer quick, efficient solutions. Offering time-saving solutions or optimizing your service to reduce time wastage can give you a competitive edge.

Effort: The Quest for Convenience

Customers value convenience and prefer solutions that require minimal effort on their part. This trend has led to the rise of on-demand services and products designed to make life easier. A Harvard Business Review study found that reducing customer effort can increase customer loyalty by up to 94%.

In the same vein as time, customers value convenience. They desire to accomplish tasks with as little effort as possible. The Corporate Executive Board (CEB) found that reducing customer effort can increase customer loyalty by 94%. Providing easy-to-use solutions and streamlining your customer service processes can effectively alleviate this pain point.

The distinction between time and effort can provide valuable insight into the opportunities for business. Below is a breakdown of The Power of Time Beyond Effort: Various Scenarios.

A Deeper Dive Into Time Vs. Effort And How It Impacts Your Money

Time refers to the duration or period spent on a particular task or activity, while effort denotes the mental or physical energy exerted

to accomplish that task. In essence, time is a measure of how long something takes, while effort represents the intensity or level of work put into completing it.

The Power of Time Beyond Effort: Various Scenarios

A person may be impacted by time without being affected by effort in several ways, such as:

- **Waiting or idle time:** When a person has to wait for an event, appointment, or result, they are impacted by the time spent waiting but not necessarily exerting any effort during that period.
- **Passive learning or entertainment:** Consuming content like watching a movie, listening to a podcast, or attending a lecture requires time investment but typically involves minimal effort from the individual.
- **Aging and natural processes:** As time passes, people naturally age and experience biological changes, regardless of the effort they put into their daily activities.
- **Observing deadlines or due dates:** Meeting a deadline, such as submitting an assignment or paying a bill, requires time management, but the time constraint itself doesn't necessarily impact the effort exerted on the task.
- **External factors or circumstances:** Sometimes, external events or situations, like traffic jams or waiting for a software update, consume time without requiring any effort from the person involved.

The Power of Effort Beyond Time: Various Scenarios

A person may be impacted by effort without being affected by time in several ways, such as:

- **The intensity of a task:** A person might quickly complete a physically or mentally demanding task, but the high level of effort required may lead to fatigue or exhaustion.
- **The quality of work:** Putting significant effort into a project or task may result in a higher quality outcome, regardless of the time spent on it. This could lead to increased satisfaction or recognition.

- **Personal growth and development:** Engaging in challenging activities that require substantial effort can lead to personal growth, skill development, and self-improvement, even if the duration of the activity is short.
- **Overcoming obstacles:** When faced with a difficult situation or problem, the effort exerted to overcome it can significantly impact the person's resilience and problem-solving abilities, independent of the time involved.
- **Physical fitness and health:** Engaging in high-intensity workouts or activities, even for a short duration, can positively impact a person's physical fitness and overall health due to the effort involved.

Health: Managing and Preventing Health Concerns

Health-related pain points constitute a significant concern for many customers. They seek assistance in managing or avoiding health issues, such as back pain, symptoms of aging, and weight loss.

Unsurprisingly, the global wellness industry is worth over $4.5 trillion, with people increasingly investing in products and services promoting better health.

Health is a primary concern for most people. As per the Centers for Disease Control and Prevention (CDC), chronic diseases, such as heart disease, cancer, and diabetes, are among the most common and costly health conditions and the most preventable. Customers are willing to pay for products or services that help them manage or avoid such health concerns.

Wealth: Earning More, Building, And Protecting Financial Assets

Customers aim to maximize the value they get for their money. They want to earn more, save where they can, get the best value for their money, and seek opportunities to maximize their financial resources. According to a Nielsen study, 84% of consumers say they're willing to switch to a brand that offers better value for money.

Wealth creation and preservation are vital pain points. According to a study by GoBankingRates, 57% of Americans have less than $1,000 in savings, indicating a pressing need for wealth-building and financial security solutions. Services like financial advisory, tax optimization, and investment strategies are areas where customers often seek professional help.

A customer focused on wealth creation is different from a customer focused on money. Customers focused on wealth aim to build generational wealth, shield themselves from negative consequences, and avoid liabilities that can impact their financial stability.

The global wealth management market is expected to reach $43.3 trillion by 2025, demonstrating customers' willingness to invest in professional advice and services to secure their financial future.

Sex: Enhancing Intimacy and Performance

Sexual health and satisfaction are essential parts of overall well-being. As per a study published in the Journal of Sexual Medicine, sexual dysfunction affects approximately 43% of women and 31% of men. Products and services that cater to improving sexual health and satisfaction have a high potential market.

Sexual satisfaction is a vital aspect of overall well-being, and customers are willing to invest in products and services that promise to improve their sex lives. The global sexual wellness market is projected to be worth $39 billion by 2024, indicating the growing demand for solutions in this area.

Security: Offering Peace of Mind

Security, encompassing both physical safety and cybersecurity, is a significant customer pain point. In an era where data breaches are prevalent, robust digital security measures are crucial to protect personal and financial data. Similarly, efficient home security solutions address safety concerns, offering peace of mind to homeowners.

For instance, a home security business providing user-friendly systems caters to the growing demand for reliable residential protection. In fact, the global home security systems market size was valued at $53.6 billion in 2020 and is expected to expand at a compound annual growth rate (CAGR) of 8.0% from 2021 to 2028. Businesses that alleviate security concerns can attract more customers and boost their revenue.

More on Security

Security can be a significant pain point for many customers in various contexts, particularly with the increased digitization of personal and financial information. Here's how it fits into the broader picture:

Security is about safeguarding both physical and digital assets. Customers want to feel safe in their transactions, interactions, and exchanges. This spans from cybersecurity to protecting personal and financial data and the physical safety of products and services. Providing robust security measures can be a significant selling point for businesses in the digital age, where data breaches and identity theft are genuine concerns.

For instance, if you're running an online store, investing in reliable and trusted security protocols (like SSL certification) will assure customers that their sensitive data (like credit card information) is safe. This alleviates their pain point of potential data theft and makes them more likely to purchase from your site.

Similarly, in a physical context, say a home security business, providing efficient and user-friendly security systems that ensure the safety of customers' homes will be addressing a primary pain point: the security of their home and family.

In both cases, by addressing security concerns (pain points), businesses can attract more customers and, in turn, increase revenue. According to Cybersecurity Ventures, cybercrime is projected to cost the world $6 trillion annually by 2021, up from $3 trillion in 2015. This rise indicates a growing need and market for security solutions.

It's important to remember that security can also relate to the stability of a job, investment, or any other situation where there's a risk of loss.

Businesses that can provide solutions that make people feel secure can often succeed.

Experiences: Living Life on Their Own Terms

Customers crave the freedom to experience life as they choose and live on their terms. They desire memorable experiences that enrich their lives and are willing to invest in them.

Customers want to travel the world, try new things, and meet new people. For example, they might be willing to pay for travel packages, event tickets, or concert tickets.

In fact, a survey by Harris Group found that 72% of millennials prefer spending more money on experiences than material things. Businesses that can provide unique, enriching experiences stand to benefit from this trend.

This trend is even evident in what the World Travel & Tourism Council travel projections. They expect travel to increase at an average rate of 5.8% annually through 2032, outpacing global GDP growth.

Providing experiences makes good business sense. According to PwC's Global Entertainment & Media Outlook, the industry is expected to grow to over $3.4 trillion by 2028, with live music and cinema contributing significantly to this expansion.

Finding the Low-Hanging Fruit Wrap-Up

In essence, recognizing and addressing these crucial customer pain points can pave the way to substantial entrepreneurial opportunities. Enterprises that successfully meet these demands earn not only customer loyalty but also access to an expansive market of consumers eager to invest in solutions that enhance their quality of life. After all, the core of successful entrepreneurship lies in delivering effective solutions.

Tips for Finding Low-Hanging Fruit to Make Money

Here are some tips on how a new entrepreneur can find easy opportunities or "low-hanging fruit" to make money in business:

- **Identify your target market.** Who are you trying to sell to? What are their needs and wants? Once you know your target market, you can start looking for opportunities to serve them.
- **Find pain points.** What problems is your target market facing? What are they struggling with? Once you know their pain points, you can start looking for ways to solve them.
- **Offer a solution.** Develop a product or service that solves the pain points of your target market. Make sure your solution is easy to use and affordable.
- **Market your product or service.** Let people know about your product or service. You can market it through online and offline channels.
- **Provide excellent customer service.** Once you have customers, make sure you provide them with excellent customer service. This will help you build customer loyalty and repeat business.

Here are some facts and figures that support these tips:

- According to a study by the Harvard Business Review, businesses that focus on solving customer pain points are 60% more likely to succeed than businesses that do not.
- A study by the Aberdeen Group found that businesses

that provide excellent customer service are 50% more likely to retain customers than businesses that do not.

- A study by the National Retail Federation found that 86% of consumers are willing to pay more for a product or service from a company that provides excellent customer service.

Following these tips can increase your chances of success as a new entrepreneur.

Here are some additional tips for finding low-hanging fruit in business:

- **Look for opportunities to improve efficiency:** Are there ways to streamline your business processes? Can you automate tasks? By improving efficiency, you can save time and money, which can free up resources to focus on other areas of your business.
- **Look for opportunities to increase sales:** Are there new markets you could enter? Can you develop new products or services? By increasing sales, you can generate more revenue, which can help you grow your business.
- **Look for opportunities to reduce costs:** Can you negotiate better deals with suppliers? Can you find ways to reduce waste? By lowering costs, you can improve your bottom line, which can make your business more profitable.

Finding and seizing low-hanging fruit can set your business up for success.

The Low-Hanging Fruit to Make Money as Experienced Entrepreneurs

Finding the "low-hanging fruit" essentially means identifying the easiest and most accessible opportunities for growth in your business. These opportunities are typically straightforward for new entrepreneurs, require fewer resources, and often yield significant returns. Here are a few strategies to consider:

Leverage Existing Customers:

According to Harvard Business Review, acquiring a new customer is anywhere from five to 25 times more expensive than retaining an existing one. So, before you look elsewhere, see if there are opportunities within your existing customer base. Can you upsell or cross-sell to them? Can you introduce a referral program to incentivize them to bring in new customers?

Improve Conversion Rates:

Improving your conversion rates can be a cost-effective way to increase your revenue. In fact, the average website conversion rate is 2.35%, but the top 10% of companies see three to five times that. Therefore, even small improvements in your conversion rate can greatly impact your bottom line. Start by analyzing your website data and identify areas for improvement.

Optimize Pricing Strategy:

Research has shown that a 1% improvement in price optimization can result in an average boost of 11.1% in profits. Therefore, re-evaluating your pricing strategy can be a quick way to improve your profitability. Test different pricing models, packages, or discount strategies to see what works best for your target market.

Diversify Your Offering:

According to a study by Bain & Company, a 5% increase in customer retention can increase a company's profitability by 75%.

One of the ways to increase customer retention is by diversifying your offerings, ensuring your business stays relevant and valuable to them.

CHAPTER 6

Uncover The Sandbox You Want to Play In And Make It Smaller

What is the best way for you to make money? It can feel overwhelming if you're just starting out. Even if you're an experienced entrepreneur, you may need to reevaluate your current business model to get you to the next business level.

No matter what type of entrepreneur you are, the concept of the 'sandbox' is a useful metaphor to describe the market or industry in which you choose to operate. However, not all sandboxes are created equal.

As an entrepreneur, uncovering the sandbox you want to play in and, importantly, making it smaller is advantageous. This process is about identifying a niche market within a broader industry that aligns with your unique skills, interests, and values. Here are some criteria to help you make the decision:

Passion and Interest:

Choose a sandbox where you have genuine interest and passion. This can fuel your motivation during challenging times and help you

stay committed for the long haul. It's easier to excel in an area you genuinely care about.

Passion and interest in a particular field or industry are not just cliché motivational concepts; they have tangible implications for business success. The Harvard Business Review revealed that founders driven by the opportunity to change the world were 30% more likely to scale their businesses than those driven by wealth. This underscores the value of passion in business growth.

As an entrepreneur, choosing a sandbox - an industry or market segment in which you have a genuine interest and passion- does more than just make the work enjoyable. It fundamentally changes your relationship with your business. Passionate entrepreneurs are more resilient, dedicated, and creative - traits that significantly contribute to business success.

Additionally, a study by Ernst and Young found that passionate entrepreneurs are more likely to attract investments. Investors recognize passion as a predictor of commitment and are, therefore, more likely to back entrepreneurs who demonstrate a passion for their businesses.

Further, having an intrinsic interest in your business area also aids in understanding your customer base better. You're more likely to understand customers' wants, needs, and expectations if you share their interests. As per the PWC's Future of Customer Experience Survey, 42% of consumers would pay more for a friendly, welcoming experience - something more readily achieved if the entrepreneur is genuinely interested in the field.

Your chosen sandbox should ideally align with your interests and passions. It makes the pathway more fulfilling, fuels motivation, enhances understanding of customer needs, and could increase

your chances of success in the long run. The facts clearly demonstrate that passion is not just an abstract concept but a real factor influencing business success.

Market Demand:

Make sure there is a real demand for the products or services you plan to offer. Conduct thorough market research to understand your potential customers' needs and wants. Here are three quick ways to jumpstart your research:

- **Google Trends:** Utilize Google Trends to explore search patterns and interests in your product or service over time. This can help you gauge the overall market demand and potential growth opportunities.
- **Conduct online surveys or polls:** Use social media platforms or survey tools to gather insights from your target audience about their needs, preferences, and willingness to buy your product or service.
- **Monitor online forums and communities:** Join relevant discussion groups, forums, or social media communities to observe the challenges, interests, and pain points of your target market.

Competition:

Assess the level of competition within your desired sandbox. A highly competitive market can be challenging for a new business. A niche market with less competition could provide you with a better starting point.

Identify successful competitors in your niche, study their offerings, and evaluate how well they are meeting the needs of the market. Look for gaps that your product or service could fill.

Profitability:

Assess potential profitability. Can you deliver your product or service at a price that people are willing to pay and that also leaves room for profit? This requires understanding the costs and pricing strategies within your chosen market.

Profitability: Assessing Potential Returns

Profitability forms the bedrock of any business venture. It's crucial to ensure that the sandbox you choose to play in offers a high potential for financial returns. This entails understanding your costs, evaluating your pricing strategies, and assessing the willingness of your target market to pay for your product or service.

Statista reports that 17% of startups fail due to pricing/cost issues, emphasizing the need for a detailed understanding of your financial dynamics. A business model that fails to take these variables into account might lead to losses instead of profits.

When assessing profitability, consider the following:

- **Cost Structure:** This involves understanding all the costs associated with delivering your product or service,including production costs, overheads, marketing, sales, distribution, and more. PwC's Global CEO Survey indicates that 62% of CEOs plan to cut costs in 2023, illustrating cost management's vital role in overall business success.
- **Pricing Strategy:** Your pricing strategy should cover your costs and provide a reasonable profit margin. McKinsey found that a 1% price increase if volumes rcmain stable, can result in an 8.7% increase in operating profits.
- **Market Willingness to Pay:** Lastly, gauge the market willingness to pay for your product or service. A report by Bain & Company shows that pricing has up to four times more impact on profitability than other business levers.

Hence, while choosing your sandbox, ensure it is a domain where you can really profit. Opt for a niche where customers see enough value in your offerings to pay a price that covers your costs and leaves room for a substantial profit.

Scalability:

Look for a sandbox where there's potential for growth. Can your business idea be expanded or replicated easily? Can it grow to serve more customers or enter new markets over time?

Scalability: The Potential for Growth

Scalability is a vital characteristic of any successful business. It defines a venture's ability to manage increasing demand and expand operations without a proportional increase in costs. In other words, it's about looking for a sandbox that allows for growth and can serve more customers or enter new markets over time.

A study by Startup Genome found that "premature scaling" is a reason why 70% of startups fail, emphasizing the importance of strategic and manageable growth.

When considering scalability, think about the following aspects:

- **Business Model Scalability:** Your business model must be designed to accommodate growth. Can your business operations be replicated, standardized, and automated to serve a larger customer base? Amazon, for instance, has exhibited scalable growth by expanding its product line, customer base, and geographic reach without significantly increasing its per-unit costs.
- **Market Size and Demand:** The potential market size and demand also determine scalability. The larger the market, the more room there is to grow. It's estimated that the global e- commerce market, for example, will be worth $6.39 trillion by 2024, showcasing its vast potential for scalability.
- **Technological Infrastructure:** Businesses with robust technological infrastructure are more likely to scale effectively. The cloud market, for instance, is projected to reach $832.1 billion by 2025, according to Gartner, indicating how technology adoption contributes to business scalability.
- **Financial Resources:** Consider whether you have access to the financial resources needed for growth. According to CB Insights, 29% of startups fail due to running out of cash, emphasizing the importance of financial planning in scaling operations.

Therefore, when choosing your sandbox, aim for a niche where you can readily scale your operations to meet growing demand without a corresponding increase in costs. This ability to scale efficiently is a critical determinant of long-term business success.

Skill and Resource Alignment:

The ideal sandbox should align with your skills, resources, and capabilities. If you lack certain key skills, consider the learning curve and the cost and feasibility of acquiring new skills. The better your abilities and assets match your business idea, the more likely you are to succeed.

A report from Gallup found that entrepreneurs who play to their strengths are three times more likely to report having an excellent quality of life, six times more likely to be engaged in their jobs, 8% more productive, and 15% less likely to quit their jobs.

Consider the following when assessing skill and resource alignment:

- **Personal Skills:** Gauge your personal skills and how they match your chosen business area. Are you technically proficient? Do you have good interpersonal skills? Can you sell? Are you a good manager? A study by the Small Business Administration found that strong leadership and management skills are common characteristics of successful entrepreneurs.
- **Experience and Expertise:** Your professional experience and expertise can significantly contribute to your venture. The British Journal of Management found that business owners with more industry experience had higher firm survival rates.
- **Learning Curve:** If you lack certain key skills, consider the learning curve and the cost and feasibility of acquiring these new skills. You could take courses, hire skilled employees, or outsource tasks. However,

remember that learning new skills takes time and energy and can increase your startup costs.

- **Financial and Physical Resources:** Make sure you have the necessary financial resources to start and sustain your business until it becomes profitable. According to the U.S. Bureau of Labor Statistics, about 20% of small businesses fail in their first year and 50% by their fifth year, often due to insufficient capital, poor credit arrangements, and an inadequate understanding of the market.
- **Network:** A robust professional network can be a valuable resource. According to LinkedIn, 80% of professionals consider networking important to career success, providing access to opportunities, knowledge, and resources.

Consequently, ensure the sandbox you're choosing to play in aligns well with your skills, resources, and capabilities. This alignment increases your chances of sustaining and growing your business in the long run.

Regulatory Environment:

Consider the industry's regulatory environment you're planning to enter. Some industries are heavily regulated and may require significant investment to ensure compliance.

By considering these factors, entrepreneurs can find the ideal sandbox - a niche market where they have a competitive edge, deliver value to customers, and enjoy financial success.

Understanding the regulatory environment of the industry you're planning to enter is crucial. Some sectors are heavily regulated and require substantial investment to ensure compliance. Non-compliance can lead to hefty fines, legal consequences, and potential damage to your business reputation.

- **Knowledge of Laws and Regulations:** Industries like healthcare, finance, and food and beverage are heavily regulated. Before entering such industries, familiarize yourself with relevant regulations. For example, the healthcare industry is governed by numerous laws like the Health Insurance Portability and Accountability Act (HIPAA). Ignorance of such regulations can lead to penalties. The Office for Civil Rights, which enforces HIPAA, settled cases with penalties as high as $5.5 million in a single case.
- **Cost of Compliance:** The cost of regulatory compliance can be substantial. A survey by Ponemon Institute found that the average cost of compliance for businesses is $5.47 million per year. This cost includes the money spent on compliance activities, technologies, and the personnel needed to carry out these activities.
- **Changing Regulations:** Regulations are dynamic, and changes can affect business operations. For instance, the introduction of the General Data Protection Regulation (GDPR) in the European Union drastically changed how businesses handle customer data, with maximum fines for non-compliance up to 4% of annual global turnover or €20 million.
- **Local Regulations:** If you're planning to operate in multiple locations, consider local regulations. Zoning laws, for instance, can dictate where certain businesses can operate. In New York City, fines for zoning law violations can range from $800 to $2,400.
- **Regulatory Support:** Some industries benefit from favorable regulations. For instance, renewable energy companies often receive government subsidies and tax incentives. In the U.S., the renewable electricity production tax credit is a per- kilowatt-hour tax credit for electricity generated by qualified energy resources.

Before choosing your sandbox, take time to research and understand the industry-specific regulations and the costs associated with them. Consult with legal experts if necessary. This proactive approach can save your business from future legal pitfalls and unnecessary expenditures.

CHAPTER 7

Test and Launch Your Business

Every successful business starts with an idea, but bringing it to life and making it profitable is the true challenge for any entrepreneur. This involves testing your idea, launching your business, and implementing strategies to generate revenue. Let's dive deeper into the essential steps and nuances of this process:

- **Prototype and MVP:** Start by developing a prototype or minimum viable product (MVP). Your MVP is the stripped- down version of your product or service that delivers the core value to your audience. It's not about perfection—it's about proof. An MVP allows you to gather insights without over investing resources. Think of it like placing a small bet to validate a big idea.

Here's a reality check: 42% of startups fail because they build something nobody wants. You're not just creating a product; you're solving a problem. Use surveys, beta testers, and soft launches to assess the true demand. Remember, customer feedback is your North Star—follow it ruthlessly.

- **Market Testing:** Market testing isn't just a "nice-to-have"—it's the proving ground for your business. Before going all-in, test your offer with real customers. Launch small-scale ad campaigns, host focus groups, or attend niche trade shows to gauge interest. For example, when Dropbox launched, they started with a demo video to test interest, not a full product.

Your goal in this phase is to fail fast and fail forward. If customers don't buy in, tweak your value proposition and try again. The faster you can iterate, the quicker you'll find a version of your product that hits the sweet spot.

- **Pricing Strategy:** Pricing isn't guesswork—it's strategy. Pricing too low devalues your product; pricing too high isolates your audience. To find the perfect price point:
    1. Benchmark competitors in your space.
    2. Understand the perceived value of your product.
    3. Experiment with dynamic pricing models.

Consider this: 70% of small businesses struggle with pricing, yet most fail to test it before launch. Use A/B testing with different price points to find what resonates. Remember, your price doesn't just reflect the cost—it signals the value you provide.

- **Business Launch:** Once you've tested and refined your product, it's time to officially launch your business. When it's time to launch, go big. But "big" doesn't always mean expensive—it means strategic. Build hype before you launch. Use teasers, countdowns, or early-access exclusives to create urgency. Companies that excel at lead nurturing generate 50% more sales at 33% lower costs. Why? Because they prime their audience before they ever make an offer.

Your launch isn't just an event—it's the start of a relationship. Use this opportunity to capture emails, build a social media following, and lay the groundwork for a loyal customer base.

- **Revenue Streams:** Single revenue streams are fragile. Imagine standing on a stool with one leg—easy to topple. Diversify your streams to stabilize your income. For example:

- ○ **Direct sales:** The obvious one.
- ○ **Subscriptions:** Predictable, recurring revenue.
- ○ **Upsells and cross-sells:** Maximize customer lifetime value.
- ○ **Affiliate partnerships:** Turn competitors into collaborators.

A Clutch survey found that 52% of small businesses rely on multiple revenue streams. It's not just about increasing profits; it's about creating a buffer against market shifts.

- **Sales and Marketing:** Post-launch, focus on building effective sales and marketing strategies to attract and retain customers. A HubSpot study found that acquiring a new customer is five times more expensive than retaining an existing one, so customer retention should be a key part of your strategy.

Sales and marketing aren't post-launch tasks—they're lifelines. A launch without a marketing plan is like opening a store in the desert. You need traffic, and traffic requires strategy. Create a marketing funnel that walks your customer from awareness to purchase.

And don't overlook retention. Acquiring a new customer costs five times more than keeping an existing one. Develop a loyalty program, send personalized follow-ups, and prioritize exceptional service to keep customers coming back.

- **Continuous Improvement:** Continue to gather customer feedback and keep improving your product or service. According to a Microsoft survey, 96% of customers say customer service is important in their choice of loyalty to a brand.

If you're not improving, you're falling behind. Listen to your customers like your business depends on it—because it does. Act on feedback to refine your product, adjust your processes, and stay ahead of the competition. The brands that win are the ones that evolve.

Here's the truth: You'll never get it perfect. But perfection isn't the goal—progress is. Keep learning, keep adapting, and keep moving forward.

Remember, launching a business is like pushing a boulder up a hill— it's hard at first, but momentum makes it easier. Test your idea rigorously, launch with intention, and refine relentlessly. Successful businesses aren't built in a day; they're built on a foundation of small wins stacked over time.

Testing and launching your business is about learning, adapting, and constantly refining your product and strategy. This proactive approach increases your chances of building a profitable business. Remember, persistence and adaptability are key attributes of successful entrepreneurship.

CHAPTER 8

Essential Tools and Resources for Online Businesses

To succeed in your online business venture, you'll need the right tools and resources to help you manage and grow your business effectively. In the following sections, we'll explore essential tools and resources for online businesses, such as website builders, payment processors, email marketing tools, social media management, and AI content tools.

These tools can give you the edge to succeed in the competitive online business world.

Website Builders

A website builder is a handy software tool that enables users to craft and maintain a website without coding skills. With a user-friendly interface and various templates and features, website builders make creating a professional-looking website for your online business easy. Some of the best website builders include Wix, Shopify, and Word-Press, offering a range of options to suit your specific needs.

When choosing a website builder, consider factors such as ease of use, customization options, and pricing. A good website builder should balance simplicity and functionality, allowing you to create a visually appealing and user-friendly website that showcases your products or services and attracts potential customers.

Payment Processors

Payment processors are essential for online businesses, enabling you to securely accept customer payments. Some of the top payment processors for online businesses include PayPal, Stripe, Square, Authorize.net, and Chase Payment Solutions. These provide a range of features and integrations to help you easily manage your online payments and uncover potential fraudulent charges.

However, considering the potential drawbacks of using payment processors, such as transaction fees and limited customer support, is essential as well.

Additionally, some payment processors may not be accessible in certain countries or regions.

Be sure to research and compare different payment processors to find the one that best suits your online business needs.

Email Marketing Tools

Email marketing is a powerful tool for online businesses, allowing you to connect with your customers and promote your products or services. Top email marketing tools for online businesses include Mailchimp, Constant Contact, Omnisend, and ConvertKit. These tools offer a variety of features and integrations to help you create effective email campaigns and track their performance.

Features like email list segmentation, automated email campaigns, and email templates can make creating engaging and targeted emails more straightforward.

Additionally, analytics features can provide valuable insights into the effectiveness of your email marketing efforts, allowing you to refine your strategy and improve your results over time.

Social Media Management

Social media management is crucial for online businesses as it allows you to manage and optimize your presence on various social media platforms. Tools such as Hootsuite, Sprout Social, AgoraPulse, and

Buffer can help you schedule and publish content, monitor and respond to comments and messages, and analyze your social media performance.

In addition to using social media management tools, developing a solid social media strategy is essential. This includes creating high-quality content that resonates with your target audience, engaging with your followers, and staying up-to-date with the latest trends and platform updates.

Using social media effectively builds relationships with customers, increases brand awareness, and ultimately grows your online business.

AI Content Tools

AI content tools are powerful software tools that use artificial intelligence to help businesses create high-quality content quickly and easily. By automating content creation tasks, such as writing, editing, and formatting, AI content tools can help companies save time and money while producing exceptional content. Some of the best AI content tools for online businesses include Copysmith, Surfer, Grammarly, ClickUp, Narrato, Lately, Jasper, Copy.ai, Synthesia, Murf, and HubSpot.

These AI content tools can help you create engaging blog posts, website content, social media posts, and more, allowing you to connect with your audience and promote your products or services effectively. By leveraging AI content tools, you can streamline your content creation process and focus on other aspects of growing your online business.

CHAPTER 9

Strategies for Growing Your Online Business

Growing your online business requires a combination of effective strategies and a commitment to continuous improvement. The first strategy to consider is creating high-quality content that resonates with your target audience. This could include blog posts, articles, videos, or social media posts that provide valuable information, entertain, or inspire your audience. By consistently producing engaging content, you can build trust and credibility with your audience, leading to increased traffic and sales.

Another crucial strategy is building relationships with your existing and potential customers. This can be achieved by engaging with them on social media, responding to comments and messages, and providing excellent customer service. By nurturing these relationships, you can create a loyal customer base that will continue to support your online business and spread the word to others.

Optimizing your online business for search engines is another key strategy for growth. This involves using search engine optimization (SEO) techniques to ensure your website and content rank highly on

search engine results pages, making it easier for potential customers to find your business. By focusing on SEO, you can increase your online visibility and attract more organic traffic to your website.

Lastly, leveraging analytics is essential for understanding the effectiveness of your online business strategies and identifying areas for improvement. Tools like Google Analytics, Facebook Insights, and email marketing platforms can provide valuable data on your website traffic, social media performance, and email marketing campaigns. By analyzing this data, you can make informed decisions on how to refine your strategies and grow your online business.

Case Studies of Successful Online Businesses

Learning from successful online businesses can be invaluable in helping you develop your own strategies and avoid common pitfalls. One inspiring case study is that of Old World Kitchen, which started as an Etsy shop selling handcrafted wooden utensils. Recognizing the limitations of the Etsy platform, the founder decided to transition to Shopify, allowing for greater control over the brand and customer experience. Today, Old World Kitchen is a thriving eCommerce business that has expanded its product line and continues to grow.

Another successful online business is Gymshark, a fitness apparel brand launched in 2012 by a 19-year-old entrepreneur with a passion for fitness and a knack for social media marketing. By leveraging the power of influencer marketing and cultivating a strong online community, Gymshark quickly grew into a multi-million-dollar business that now competes with major players in the fitness apparel industry.

These case studies demonstrate the power of perseverance, innovation, and strategic thinking in achieving success in the world of online businesses. By learning from their experiences and applying their strategies to your own online business, you, too, can achieve remarkable results and make your mark in the digital realm.

By exploring various online business ideas, considering key criteria, and leveraging essential tools and resources, you can create a thriving online business that aligns with your skills, interests, and lifestyle. With a strong foundation and a commitment to continuous improvement, you can achieve financial freedom and the satisfaction of owning your own business.

In this book, we've drilled down to the essentials of making money online. We've explored everything from online business basics to dissecting the most profitable models. My goal has been to provide you with practical advice, strategies, and resources that will help boost your profits and successfully navigate the world of online business. Consider this book a valuable tool in your entrepreneurial toolbox, and remember that building a successful online business is not just about making money - it's also about creating value for your customers.

Now is the perfect time to take the leap and embrace the limitless potential of the online business world.

I hope you've enjoyed listening to this book, as a reminder, you can access the tables, bonus content, and other resources on our companion website.

Simply head over to eLuminateNetwork.com, and you'll find all the visual materials organized by book chapter for easy navigation. Additionally, this site is home to our exclusive bonus content, which I'm sure you'll find beneficial as you progress on your entrepreneurial journey. So, whether you're looking for tables, graphs, or that extra information to push your business forward, remember it's all just a click away.

Let's continue this journey to online entrepreneurial success together!

———

Closing Thoughts...
A Final Note from S.R. Brown

YOU MADE IT! How to Make Money in Business Online is more than a book, it's a roadmap to your next level. By reaching this point, you've shown you're ready to take action, think bigger, and build something extraordinary.

Now, I have one last request: Pay it forward.

Scan the QR code below to leave a review on Amazon. Your feedback not only helps me improve but also fuels other entrepreneurs on their journey to success. Together, we're building a community of doers, dreamers, and game- changers.

The next move is yours—make it count. Keep winning,

S.R. Brown

Unstoppable Profit
for Business Owners

CAPTURE ATTENTION, DRIVE SALES, AND ACHIEVE BREAKTHROUGH GROWTH USING BATTLE-TESTED STRATEGIES FROM ONE OF HISTORY'S GREATEST ENTREPRENEURS

S.R. Brown

Unstoppable Profit for Business Owners

Copyright © 2025 by Halcyon Enterprise Inc.

All rights reserved.

Disclaimer

The information provided in this book is for educational and informational purposes only. While the author has made every effort to ensure accuracy, the strategies and advice presented are based on the author's research, experience, and opinions. Results may vary depending on individual circumstances, market conditions, and business contexts.

This book does not constitute professional business, financial, or legal advice. Readers are encouraged to consult with qualified professionals before making significant business decisions or implementing strategies discussed in this work.

The author and publisher assume no responsibility for errors, omissions, or outcomes resulting from the application of information contained herein. Any perceived slight of specific people, companies, or organizations is unintentional.

Book 2 Contents:
Unstoppable Profit
for Business Owners

Introduction

Battle-Tested Entrepreneurship Principles That Show You How To Make Money, Build Wealth, and Scale Your Business

Before Steve Jobs was selling a vision from a stage, before Sara Blakely cut the feet off pantyhose and created a billion-dollar brand, and before a single influencer monetized their personal brand, there was Phineas Taylor Barnum.

And he faced the same battles you do today: sleepless nights wondering if his product would find its market, the crushing weight of payroll when revenue dipped, the constant fight for attention in a crowded marketplace, and the temptation to chase every shiny opportunity that crossed his path.

Before you dismiss PT Barnum as "just a circus guy," consider that when he died in 1891, his net worth exceeded $300 million in today's dollars. He built this fortune not once, but three times, rebuilding wealth from complete financial ruin twice. He created America's first viral marketing campaigns, pioneered customer experience design, and turned his personal brand into a global phenomenon.

Most importantly, he left behind a blueprint, a precise set of operational principles that work as well today as they did during his time.

Timeless Business Principles

This book expands upon the time-tested rules that Barnum built into a practical system for modern entrepreneurs. Each principle addresses a core challenge every founder faces:

Foundation Principles (Chapters 1-3):
1. Find Your Founder-Market Fit
2. Choose Your Strategic Location
3. Master Smart Capital

Growth Principles (Chapters 4-8): 4. Engineer Attention and Demand 5. Create Customer Evangelists 6. Develop Unbreakable Persistence 7. Stay Connected to Your Core Business 8. Build an Unassailable Reputation

Scale Principles (Chapters 9-10): In the remaining chapters, you'll focus on key concepts, such as ways to maintain laser focus, avoid speculative distractions. It's about creating systems that work without you and building your information advantage.

Legacy Principles: There are also legacy principles such as invest in quality tools and people creating purpose beyond profit, and protecting your strategic advantages.

Why These Principles Work Now More Than Ever

Today's entrepreneurs face the same fundamental challenges Barnum did, just with different tools:

The Attention Economy: Barnum competed for attention on crowded city streets. You compete for it in crowded social media feeds.

The Trust Deficit: Barnum had to overcome skepticism about his "curiosities." You must overcome skepticism about your startup's or product's bold claims.

The Scale Challenge: Barnum needed systems to manage a traveling circus with hundreds of employees. You need systems to scale a remote team across time zones.

The principles remain constant. Only the applications change. Barnum was writing the playbook on gaining visibility while he was building his empire.

- **He was the visionary of viral marketing before the concept of a "going viral" was even a thing.**
  When he marched his elephants, including the world-

famous Jumbo, across the newly opened Brooklyn Bridge, it was a calculated media stunt that generated millions of dollars in free press. He didn't pay for ads; he created an event so compelling the newspapers had no choice but to cover it.

- **He practically invented FOMO (Fear Of Missing Out).** His advertisements were masterpieces of urgency and scarcity. Attractions were for a "limited time only." He sold a ticket not just to a show, but to a cultural moment you couldn't afford to miss. This is the same psychological driver behind every limited-edition sneaker drop and flash sale today.
- **He was a master of the pivot.** When one venture failed, he didn't quit; he absorbed the lessons and applied them to his next project. He understood that failure wasn't a verdict but lessons learned for his education in business.
- **He understood that the customer experience *is* the product.** Barnum knew the show began on the street, with the banners, the music, and the grand entrance. He obsessed over every detail that would transport his customer's lives into something much more interesting.

How to Use This Book

Each chapter follows the same structure:

1. **The Timeless Principle** - Original business insights that have stood the test of time

2. **The Modern Translation** - Business rules that apply to today's business environment

3. **The Action Framework** - Specific steps you can implement immediately

4. **The Success Metrics** - How to measure if it's working

This isn't theory. It's a field manual tested by over a century of entrepreneurial success and boiled down to essential business take-aways that every entrepreneur needs to put into practice.

Preface

While most entrepreneurs chase the latest growth hacks and funding strategies, this book delivers something far more valuable: principles that have been making entrepreneurs wealthy for generations. The companies that build lasting wealth don't rely on trends, they master a small set of fundamental principles.

That's what makes this different: This book contains the operational foundations that turn ambitious ideas into money-making enterprises, not trendy tactics that work for six months. When you understand why Amazon obsesses over customer experience, why Patagonia's integrity drives billion-dollar loyalty, and why Dropbox's viral growth felt effortless, you're seeing these timeless principles in action.

P.T. Barnum's *The Art of Money Getting*, written over 150 years ago, contains the most practical business advice ever written. Barnum built a $300 million fortune (in today's dollars) not once, but three times, recovering from complete bankruptcy twice. He pioneered viral marketing, invented FOMO, and mastered customer experience design, all before these concepts had names.

The problem? Barnum's original text was written for shopkeepers and traveling circuses. The principles were timeless, but the applications needed translation for today's entrepreneurs. This book solves that problem. I've spent two decades testing Barnum's strategies and seeing them in action with modern entrepreneurs. This book distills his original twenty rules into the fifteen most critical principles for today's business landscape. The results have been remarkable: businesses implementing these strategies see dramatic improvements in customer retention, revenue growth, profitability, and operational efficiency.

Why Barnum, Why Now

P.T. Barnum understood something most entrepreneurs miss: building wealth isn't about chasing the latest trend, it's about mastering fundamentals that never change. His principles survived the Industrial Revolution, the Information Age, and are proving essential in the AI Revolution because they're based on unchanging human psychology and sound business fundamentals.

The tools change, but the principles remain constant. Whether you're launching a tech startup or opening a local business, these fifteen strategies provide the proven roadmap from startup to empire.

Barnum's blueprint for success is waiting in the pages that follow. Your job is to put it into practice.

CHAPTER 1

Find Your Founder-Market Fit

"Your greatest strength becomes your best path to success."

The #1 reason startups fail isn't always lack of capital or market timing. It's founder-market mismatch. You can have the best business idea in the world, but if you're not the right person to execute it, you'll fail.

Consider this: every year, thousands of entrepreneurs launch the "next Uber for this" or "Airbnb of that", but even with solid market research, adequate funding, and technically sound business plans 90% fail within the first year. Why does this happen? The idea wasn't wrong, the execution was. Think about it: even the most brilliant logistics concept launched by someone who hates operations is doomed for failure from the start. The entrepreneur behind the idea will likely just crumble under the weight of daily management challenges. If the next great social app is built by an introvert who struggles with community building, it will never achieve the viral growth it needs.

The harsh reality is that markets don't care about your good intentions or how much you've invested. The customers in those markets respond to execution. But here's what most entrepreneurs miss: execution requires you to operate within your zone of genius and pull from your natural strengths. No, this doesn't mean that you have to be the one doing it all, but you need founder-market fit so you can execute for years at a time, through countless setbacks and pivots. Founder-market fit must be your first priority. When you're fighting both the market and your own limitations, failure becomes inevitable.

When Drew Houston forgot his USB drive on a bus ride from

Boston to New York in 2007, he turned his frustration into action and started coding a solution on the spot. That impromptu coding session became Dropbox. The result? A billion-dollar company that solved a problem millions experienced.

Houston wasn't just another entrepreneur chasing a trend; he was a programmer who lived the daily pain of file syncing across multiple devices. His technical skills, personal frustration, and deep understanding of the problem created perfect founder-market fit.

This same principle of alignment between personal strengths and market opportunity drove PT Barnum's success over a century earlier, though he had to learn it through painful failure first.

As a young man, Barnum tried being a shopkeeper. He was miserable and unsuccessful. Why? Because his genius wasn't in quiet behind-the-scenes sales, it was in spectacular promotion. The moment he aligned his vision with his natural talents, he became unstoppable.

The Number One Question To Ask

Building a business will test the very limits of your passion, resilience, and skill. Before you write a line of code, design a logo, or scout a location, the most crucial question you must answer has nothing to do with the market, but with yourself: *Are you the right person for this journey?*

This is the principle of **Founder-Market Fit**. It's the powerful alignment between your innate talents, your deepest interests, and a genuine, addressable need in the world. Lasting, meaningful success is rarely found by chasing a trend or entering a field simply because it seems lucrative. It is built by people who are operating in their natural element, a place where their work feels less like a job and more like a calling.

Understanding Product-Market Fit

Founder-Market Fit is the essential prerequisite for achieving its more famous cousin: **Product-Market Fit (PMF)**. Coined by venture capitalist Marc Andreessen, Product-Market Fit means "being in a good market with a product that can satisfy that market." It is the moment when you have built something that a critical mass of people genuinely wants and needs.

You can *feel* the difference between having it and not having it:

- **Before PMF:** You feel like you are pushing a massive boulder uphill. Growth is slow and expensive. Customer acquisition is a grind. You spend all your time trying to convince people they need your product. Word of mouth is non-existent.
- **After PMF:** You feel like you are being pulled by an unstoppable force. Customers are finding you. Usage is growing organically. The product is selling itself because it so perfectly solves a real-world problem. You can't respond to the inbound demand fast enough.

Achieving this requires a deep, almost obsessive understanding of a specific market's pain points. And this is why Founder-Market Fit is so critical.

Barnum saw countless people abandon a natural talent for businesses they were ill-suited for, only to fail. A person with a brilliant mechanical mind might throwaway their gift to become a mediocre retailer, simply because they saw others getting rich in that field. The result was almost always unhappiness and financial ruin.

We see this play out constantly today. A talented artist decides to launch a complex fintech company because they see the high valuations in the tech industry. They soon find themselves drowning in spreadsheets and regulatory compliance, fields for which they have no natural aptitude or interest. Their initial vision is lost, their energy drains, and the venture stalls. The world didn't gain a great fintech product; it lost a brilliant artist. They are, as Barnum would say, a "fish out of water."

The Founder-Market Fit Framework

Most entrepreneurs focus on Product-Market Fit first. That's backwards. You need Founder Market Fit before you can achieve sustainable Product-Market Fit.

Founder-Market Fit =
Your Zone of Genius + Market Opportunity + Personal
Passion

Let's break this down:

Step 1: Identify Your Zone of Genius

Your Zone of Genius isn't what you're good at, it's what you're uniquely excellent at. Answer these questions:

Energy Audit:

- What activities make you lose track of time?
- What problems do you solve that others find difficult?
- When do people naturally come to you for advice?

Pattern Recognition:

- What have you been consistently good at across different jobs/situations?
- What do colleagues always ask you to handle?
- What type of problems do you instinctively understand?

Barnum's Zone of Genius was the orchestration of public attention. He could create curiosity from nothing, turn spectacle into education, and make people feel part of something larger than themselves.

Step 2: Map Market Opportunities

Your genius is only valuable if there's market demand for it. Look for:

Pain Points You Naturally Understand:

- What frustrations do you experience that others share?
- What industries or problems fascinate you?
- Where do you see obvious solutions others miss?

Growing Market Demand:

- Is this problem getting bigger or smaller?
- Are more people experiencing this pain?
- Is the current solution inadequate?

Step 3: Test for Authentic Passion

Passion isn't about what excites you, it's about what you can sustain through inevitable difficulties.

The Persistence Test:

- Would you work on this problem for free?
- Can you see yourself doing this for 10+ years?
- Does thinking about this market energize or drain you?

The Three Founder-Market Fit Types

Based on patterns from hundreds of successful entrepreneurs, there are three primary ways founders align with their markets:

The Domain Expert

- **Profile:** Deep industry experience reveals unique insights
- **Example:** A former restaurant manager who builds software specifically for restaurant operations
- **Advantage:** Knows customer pain intimately, speaks their language, has built-in credibility

The Personal Pain Solver

- **Profile:** Builds solution to their own frustrating problem

- **Example:** A frequent traveler who creates a better expense management app
- **Advantage:** Is their own ideal customer, deeply motivated to solve the problem

The Skill Transferrer

- **Profile:** Applies unique expertise to a new market
- **Example:** A game designer who applies gamification principles to employee training
- **Advantage:** Brings fresh perspective, sees opportunities others miss

Action Framework: The 30-Day Founder-Market Fit Assessment

Week 1: Self-Audit

- Complete the Zone of Genius diagnostic above
- Interview 5 people who know your work well - ask them what you're uniquely good at
- List every problem/industry you find genuinely interesting

Week 2: Market Research

- For each interesting area, spend 2 hours researching market size, growth, and current solutions
- Identify 3-5 potential problem areas that meet both genius and market criteria Eliminate anything that doesn't genuinely excite you

Week 3: Customer Discovery

- For remaining opportunities, interview 10 potential customers about their pain points

- Ask: "What's the most frustrating part of [your situation]?"
- Listen for problems that make you think: "I could solve that"

Week 4: Passion Validation

- Choose the top 2 opportunities
- Spend 10 hours working on each (research, prototype, design)
- Pay attention to your energy levels - which one energizes vs. drains you?

Red Flags: When You're Forcing the Fit

The Trend Chaser: You're pursuing an opportunity because it's hot, not because it matches your strengths.

- *Warning sign:* You struggle to explain why you're the right person for this market

The Skill Misaligner: You're trying to build something that requires skills you don't have and don't enjoy developing.

- *Warning sign:* The core work feels like a constant uphill battle

The Passion Faker: You're intellectually interested but not emotionally committed.

- *Warning sign:* You find yourself procrastinating on important business tasks

Success Metrics: How to Measure Founder-Market Fit
You'll know you have strong Founder-Market Fit when:
Internal Indicators:

- You can work on this problem for hours without fatigue
- Discussing your market with others comes naturally and enthusiastically
- You find yourself reading about this industry in your spare time

External Indicators:

- Potential customers immediately understand why you're building this
- Industry experts take your insights seriously
- You can explain complex market dynamics simply

Business Indicators:

- Customer acquisition feels more like education than persuasion
- You naturally attract advisors and talent from this space
- Your solution evolves quickly based on your instinctive understanding

Case Study: Founder-Market Fit in Action

Barnum's path to founder-market fit was not through a single job title like "museum owner" or "circus operator." He tapped into his unique genius, to be a master orchestrator of public attention.

He was, at his core, a marketer and influencer of the masses. He understood, better than anyone, what made people stop, look, and, most importantly, talk. His calling was a unique fusion of three distinct talents:

1. Driving Attention:

It's no secret that the greatest product in the world is worthless if no one knows it exists. Barnum's genius was in creating curiosity out of thin air. A famous (and possibly embellished) story illustrates this perfectly: to drive traffic to his museum, he once hired a man to simply lay bricks one by one on a street corner near the entrance, then carry them across the street and repeat the process, which drew a huge crowd of curiosity seekers. When the crowd became large enough, the man would walk through the front door of the museum, and some of the crowd would end up paying the admission fee to follow him inside to see what would happen next. This type of crowd build-up was Barnum's focus—not laying bricks, but under- standing that a public interest is the best advertisement.

2. Blurring the Lines of Entertainment and Education:

Barnum recognized that the public wanted to feel that they were improving themselves while being entertained. He found success in masterfully walking the line between interest and entertainment. For example, he didn't just have singers and actors present; he created a "Lecture Room" where "moral dramas" were performed. This allowed him to attract a family audience that would not have had an interest in just a regular theater performance, which helped dramatically expand his market.

3. Creating Shared Experiences:

More than anything, Barnum understood that people crave being part of a shared cultural event. He was successful at taking private attractions and making them into public phenomena. He didn't just transport his famous elephant, Jumbo, to the circus; he announced that Jumbo would walk across the new Brooklyn Bridge to "test its structural integrity." This turned a simple logistical act into a city-wide spectacle that dominated news- papers for days. He wasn't selling an elephant; he was selling a story that everyone in New York could participate in and talk about.

Defining Entrepreneurial Moment

Barnum found his calling. He instantly created a product with staggering market fit when purchased the struggling American Museum when he was just 31 years old. The purchase was not a simple transaction; it was a defining entrepreneurial moment that shaped his future success. The museum was a dusty, poorly-managed collection of curiosities. Barnum had no capital of his own to buy it, so he had to rely entirely on his wits and reputation. He convinced the current owner to sell it to him on credit, effectively making a highly leveraged bet on his own ability to turn the business around. This single, audacious move marked his transition from a wandering jack-of-all-trades to a focused, stationary business owner in the heart of New York City.

The "product" was the museum itself. The "market" was a public hungry for novelty, entertainment, and a sense of educational wonder. Barnum's genius for promotion (the Founder fit) allowed him to create a product (the museum experience) that the market couldn't get enough of. He didn't have to push a boulder; he simply opened the doors, and the public pulled his venture to incredible heights.

How PT Barnum achieved perfect Founder-Market Fit:

- **Zone of Genius:** Master of public attention that instinctively knew what made people stop, stare, and talk.
- **Market Opportunity:** Capitalized on a public hungry for performance and educational entertainment in an era with few entertainment options.
- **Personal Passion:** Genuine obsession with creating opportunities that transported people from their mundane lives into extraordinary experiences.

The result? He transformed a failing museum into America's most popular attraction, drawing 38 million visitors when the entire U.S. population at the time was only 31 million.

Your Next Action

Before you move to the next chapter, build your action plan. Write a one-paragraph "Founder-Market Fit Statement" that follows this template:

"I am uniquely positioned to solve [specific problem] for [specific market] because I have [unique insight/skill/experience]. This market needs this solution because [pain point/trend]. I am passionate about this because [personal connection]."

Here's an education technology example:

I'm uniquely positioned to solve the challenge of personalized math learning for middle school students in underserved communities because I have eight years of experience as a math teacher in Title 1 schools and a background in adaptive learning technology,

This market needs this solution because 60% of students in these communities fall behind in math by seventh grade, creating a critical gap that affects future opportunities. I'm passionate about this because I was once a struggling math student myself and one dedicated teacher changed how I feel about math for the rest of my life.

If you can't complete this statement confidently, return to the assessment framework. Everything else in this book builds on getting this foundation right.

Remember Barnum's warning: "A fish out of water" will never succeed, no matter how hard it tries. But a fish in its natural element becomes unstoppable.

Find your water first. Everything else follows.

CHAPTER 2

Select the Right Location: Your Digital and Physical "Place"

After you have aligned your business with your natural genius, your Founder-Market Fit, one of your next critical decisions is about where to plant your flag. P.T. Barnum dedicated an entire rule to this: "Select The Right Location." For him, this meant choosing the right town and the right street corner. He knew that a brilliant business idea could fail completely if it was hidden in a place where no customers could find it. 'You might conduct your business with a repeatable and reproducible process,' he warned, "and yet, if you were located in a remote village where customers were few and far between, your business would be small and your profits unimportant."

This bit of advice is more relevant today than ever, but the meaning of "location" has expanded dramatically. Your location is no longer just a physical address; it is a strategic port- folio of presence, both in the physical world and across the vast, complex digital domain. A poor location strategy, whether on a quiet side street or on page ten of Google search results, will render even the most brilliant business invisible.

Physical Locations Without a "Customer Deficit"

Let's first acknowledge that for many businesses, physical location may be essential. If you are opening a restaurant, a retail store, a fitness studio, or a local service company, the classic rules still apply with an iron grip. Pay a higher rent for a location with more foot traffic is not an expense; it's an investment in marketing. That busy street corner is a 24/7 advertisement for your business.

Consider two coffee shops: One is located on a bustling main street, steps from a subway station. The other is two blocks away on a quiet residential street, offering a slightly better product at a slightly lower price. The main street location will almost certainly outperform the other, capturing customers through sheer convenience and visibility. The second shop is forced to spend significant time and money on marketing just to make people aware that it exists. It has chosen a location with a "customer deficit."

Before you sign a lease, apply Barnum's principles to the physical world:

Go Where You Are Needed: Don't open the fifth yoga studio on a single block. As Barnum noted, the man who has a trade to himself will make a fortune, while the one who has to compete with a dozen others will struggle. Look for "commercial deserts"; areas with a clear need for what you offer.

Visibility is a Currency: A location hidden from view is a location that doesn't exist to the casual customer. Is it easy to find? Is there parking? Is it in a place your ideal customer already frequents? Answering these questions correctly is the first step in engineering success.

The Digital Domain: Your Place on the Internet

For the modern entrepreneur, the most critical location is often digital. The internet is not one single "place"; it is a universe of distinct cities, streets, and marketplaces. Choosing the right ones is the new art of location strategy.

1. Your Digital Marketplace "Location"

Where will your business digitally "live"? This choice dictates the rules you must follow, the customers you can reach, and the competition you will face.

The Mega-Mall (Amazon, Alibaba): Setting up shop on Amazon gives you access to an unbelievable amount of foot traffic. However, you are renting a small kiosk in a massive mall. You must pay their "rent" (fees), abide by their rules, and compete with thousands of other vendors shouting for attention just steps away from you.

The Artisan Market (Etsy, Upwork): Platforms like Etsy cater to specific niches (handmade goods, vintage items), while platforms like Upwork cater to freelancers. These locations offer a more targeted audience that is already looking for what you sell, but your total addressable market is smaller.

The App Store (Apple & Google): If your product is a mobile application, you live and die by the rules and algorithms of these powerful gatekeepers. Getting featured is like getting prime real estate on Fifth Avenue; being buried in search is like being in a locked basement.

Your Own Sovereign Territory (Direct-to-Consumer Website): Building your own e-commerce site (e.g., via Shopify or Squarespace) is like buying your own land and constructing your own building. You have total control over the brand, the customer experience, and the data, for the most part. However, you have no built-in traffic. You are responsible for building every road that leads customers to your door.

2. Your Social Platform: Choosing Your "Street Corner"

If your website is your store, social media platforms are the streets where your customers hang out. You cannot be on every street corner. You must choose wisely, planting your flag where your target audience congregates.

The Professional Hub (LinkedIn): For a B2B consulting firm or a SaaS company, LinkedIn is the essential location. It's the digital equivalent of a downtown business district.

The Visual Square (Instagram & TikTok): For a fashion brand, a restaurant, or any business that relies on aesthetics and culture, these platforms are non-negotiable. This is the trendy, bustling neighborhood where visual trends are born.

The Community Hall (Facebook & Reddit): For businesses that thrive on community engagement and niche interests (local services, hobby groups), these platforms are the town squares and community centers of the internet.

Barnum's wisdom directly applies: "Go where you are wanted." Don't waste your energy trying to sell enterprise software on TikTok or vintage clothing on LinkedIn. Meet your customers in their chosen location.

3. The Global Main Street: The Front Page of Google

Ultimately, the most valuable real estate in the digital world is the first page of a Google search. Search Engine Optimization (SEO) is the modern science of securing a prime location. Being on page one for a relevant search term is the equivalent of having a flagship store with a giant, glowing sign on the busiest street in the world. Being on page two or beyond is, as Barnum would say, being "in a remote village where customers are few and far between."

The Hybrid Strategy: Blending Clicks and Bricks

The most successful businesses of our time master the hybrid approach. They understand that digital and physical locations are not separate but deeply interconnected.

A local restaurant uses targeted Instagram ads (**digital location**) to show photos of its food to people within a five-mile radius, driving them to its tables (**physical location**).

A direct-to-consumer clothing brand like Allbirds, which started online (**digital location**), opens physical showrooms in major cities (**physical location**) to allow customers to touch the product, strengthening the brand and driving more online sales.

Your task as a founder is to see this entire map (physical and digital) and strategically place your outposts. Don't think of location as a single choice. Think of it as a network. Where will you be found? Where will you engage? Where will you transact?

The principle has not changed since Barnum's day. To succeed, you must be seen. You must be accessible. You must be in the right place at the right time. Whether that place is a storefront on Main Street or the top of a search query, the rule remains the same:

choose your location wisely, for it is the foundation upon which your entire enterprise will be built.

CHAPTER 3

Avoid Bad Debt: Smart Capital and Sustainable Growth

The world of venture capital, angel investors, and readily available credit, the idea of "avoiding debt" can seem like unrealistic advice. Startups are built on "Other People's Money" (OPM), and the billion-dollar "unicorns" that dominate headlines are often powered by massive infusions of outside capital. In this context, P.T. Barnum's stern warning; 'The borrower is always indebted to the lender'can sound hopelessly out of date.

But to dismiss it is to miss the profound and timeless principle at its core. Barnum's thinking was not a simplistic command to never borrow. It was more like a razor-sharp distinction between two fundamentally different types of capital: the kind that serves you and the kind that overwhelms you.

"Money is in some respects like fire," he wrote. The question for the modern founder, is not whether to use the fire of OPM, but whether you are in control of the flame. The entire art of entrepreneurial finance lies in knowing when capital is a tool that builds your freedom and when it is a chain that ensures your servitude.

Desperation Debt: When Borrowing Fails

The debt that Barnum railed against with such fury is what we can call "desperation debt." This is money borrowed not from a position of strength and opportunity, but from a position of weakness and fear. It is debt taken on to fill a hole, not to build a bridge.

Borrowing to cover operational losses:

Using loans or credit cards to make payroll or pay rent because your business is not generating enough cash is the financial equivalent of treading water in a hurricane. You are not solving the underlying problem; you are merely delaying the inevitable drowning while going deeper into the red.

High-interest consumer debt:

Funding your startup on personal credit cards is the fastest path to ruin. The compounding interest creates a financial headwind that makes success nearly impossible.

Borrowing without a clear, predictable ROI:

Taking on debt for vanity projects, such as a lavish office or speculative marketing, without a direct line of sight to how it will generate more revenue than it costs is pure nonsense or "folly" (as it would be called in that time).

Barnum himself learned this lesson in the most painful way imaginable. In the mid 1850s, long after his initial success, he was persuaded to endorse promissory notes for the Jerome Clock Company, a venture he did not control or operate. He essentially co-signed their loans, lending his good name to their enterprise. When the company collapsed, its creditors came for Barnum. He was legally on the hook for a fortune. This single act of foolish- ness, of taking on debt for an operation outside his control, nearly destroyed him. It dragged him through a humiliating public bankruptcy and years of struggle. He had willingly made a bad decision that nearly cost him everything.

Opportunity Capital: When Debt Builds

In stark contrast to this is "opportunity capital." This is money borrowed from a position of strength, for a specific, strategic purpose that is designed to generate a return far greater than its cost. This is the "excellent servant." It is not a chain but a lever, allowing you to achieve a result that would be impossible with your resources alone.

The greatest example of this is the very act that launched

Barnum's career. When he saw the massive opportunity: to purchase the struggling American Museum in New York City. He knew, with absolute certainty that he could transform it into a cash-generating machine. But he had no money.

Did he walk away? No. He executed a brilliant leveraged buyout. He convinced the owner to sell him the museum entirely on credit, using the future proceeds of the museum itself as collateral. This was an immense debt. By his own rigid definition, he was deciding to play with fire. But he wasn't.

In this case, he was using debt as a tool. He was borrowing to acquire a severely undervalued, cash-producing asset for which he had a clear and brilliant turnaround plan. The debt was not a desperate act to cover a loss; it was a strategic move to secure an opportunity. The income generated by his revitalized museum quickly dwarfed the cost of his debt service, making him a wealthy man. He had mastered the fire and used it to forge an empire.

Understanding "Dumb Money"

Barnum's "fire" metaphor is what we now call Dumb Money. This is capital that comes with ruinous terms, strips you of control, and fundamentally misaligns your business with your goals.

Dumb Money often looks like this:

High-Interest Consumer Debt: The most dangerous form is funding your startup on personal credit cards. The crushing interest rates (often exceeding 20%) create a financial headwind that is nearly impossible to overcome. You are not just building a business; you are trying to outrun an avalanche of compounding debt. This is the quickest path to both business failure and personal bankruptcy.

Predatory Loans: These are loans with opaque terms, hidden fees, and aggressive repayment schedules that are designed to profit from your potential failure. They prey on desperation and are the modern equivalent of the loan sharks Barnum warned against.

Desperate Equity Rounds: This happens when a founder, facing a cash crunch, takes money from any investor who will offer it. The result is selling off huge percentages of your company for a relatively small amount of cash. You may have saved the business for a few months, but you've sacrificed your future. You are no longer the primary owner of your own idea; you are a minority shareholder working for your investors and you don't have a solid plan to build longterm equity because you were only focused on a short-term cash infusion.

The common thread is a loss of control. Whether to a credit card company or a predatory investor, you are no longer making decisions based on what is best for the product or the customer, but on how to satisfy your short-term financial need.

The Art of "Smart Capital"

Smart Capital, on the other hand, is a strategic tool. It is capital acquired on favorable terms to achieve a specific, strategic goal that will generate a return far greater than its cost. The ultimate smart capital includes:

1. Bootstrapping

The purest expression of Barnum's ideal is bootstrapping. This means starting small, funding your initial operations from your own savings, and then relentlessly reinvesting your profits back into the business to fuel growth. Companies like Mailchimp, Basecamp, and GitHub all started this way, growing into billion-dollar giants without taking on early venture capital.

Bootstrapping forces discipline. It demands you create a product that customers will pay for from day one. It ensures you maintain 100% control over your vision and your destiny. It is Barnum's advice in its most literal and powerful form: "Let your expenses be less than your receipts." Start small and let the business itself fund its own expansion.

2. Strategic Debt

Not all debt is dumb. Strategic debt is borrowing for a precise purpose that unlocks growth. Think of an e-commerce business taking out a Small Business Administration (SBA) loan to purchase inventory in bulk at a 30% discount. The interest on the loan is a fraction of the savings, leading to higher profit margins. Or consider a photography business taking a loan to buy a new camera that allows it to book higher-paying clients.

The key is that the debt is tied to a clear, predictable return on investment. You are not borrowing to cover losses; you are investing in an asset or opportunity that will pay for itself many times over.

3. Venture Capital and Angel Investors

Venture Capital (VC) is the most misunderstood form of funding. It is selling shares, not your soul, and it's not a loan. It is selling a piece of your company. The "cost" is not interest; it is equity, board seats, and immense pressure to grow at an exponential rate.

This is where Barnum's wisdom is most crucial. Taking on VC money is only "smart" if you are building a very specific type of business, one capable of generating a 10x or 100x return for your investors. If your goal is to build a wonderful, profitable "lifestyle business" that makes you a few hundred thousand dollars a year, taking VC money is a catastrophic mistake. Their definition of success (a billion-dollar exit) and yours are fundamentally misaligned.

Smart Capital from an investor isn't just cash. It's capital that comes with a network, expertise, and mentorship. A "smart" investor, when done right, is a true strategic partner who can open doors and help you avoid common pitfalls. A "dumb" investor simply gives you a check and then demands reports and results. Before you take a dollar of venture capital, ask: "Am I just getting a check, or am I getting a co-pilot?"

The Unchanging Rule: Profit is King

Whatever your capital strategy, bootstrapping, strategic debt, or venture funding, it must lead to a single destination: a sustainable, profitable business model. Cash flow is the lifeblood. Profit is the proof that you are creating more value than you are consuming. Barnum built his empire by obsessing over the simple math of income versus expenses. This focus is the ultimate antidote to the siren song of "growth at all costs." Growth without a path to profitability is just a faster way to go broke.

Before you seek funding, create a plan. Understand exactly how you need to use that capital to create a profitable, durable business. Remember the core lesson: money is a tool. A tool you must master. Use it to build your vision, not to blindly link yourself to the vision of others. Your goal is not merely to get funding, but to build a business that is fundamentally capable of scaling. That is the true art of money making.

CHAPTER 4

Advertise Your
Business: Mastering

P.T. Barnum understood a truth so fundamental it is shocking how many entrepreneurs ignore it: a great product in hiding is worthless. He saw business owners who would "stand shivering on the brink of prosperity," too timid to invest in letting the public know they existed. He compared them to a man who, having lit a candle, immediately hides it under a bushel. "The public," Barnum thundered, "is a very curious customer, and if you do not let it know that you have what it wants, it will never find you out."

This is the cardinal sin of modern business: the sin of invisibility. We live in an age of infinite noise and distraction. Obscurity is the default state. To build a successful enterprise today, you cannot simply open your doors (physical or digital) and expect customers to find you. You must, as Barnum did, become a master of capturing attention. You must advertise.

From Print to Pixels: Choosing Your Medium

Barnum's primary tools were the newspaper and the printed poster. He would blanket a town with "printer's ink" to announce the arrival of his circus. He bought ad space, wrote compelling copy, and created a buzz that was impossible to ignore. Today, the "town square" is digital, and the tools are infinitely more varied and powerful. Your job is to master them.

Content Marketing & SEO (The New Newspaper):
When people in Barnum's day had a need, they might look to the local paper. Today, they go to Google. Search Engine Optimiza-

tion (SEO) is the art and science of being the top answer when your potential customer asks a question. This isn't just about keywords; it's about creating genuinely useful content, like blog posts, guides, videos, and tools that establishes your authority. By giving value upfront, you become the trusted resource, the digital "light on a hill" that search engines and customers flock to.

Social Media (The Modern Poster):

Platforms like Instagram, TikTok, Facebook, and LinkedIn are the modern equivalents of Barnum's illustrated posters. They are visual, immediate, and can spread with incredible speed. But simply posting is not enough. You must understand the culture of each platform. A professional, case-study-driven post on LinkedIn will fail on TikTok, where irreverent, fast paced video reigns supreme. As Barnum chose his ad placements with care, you must choose your platforms with precision, creating native content that feels like part of the conversation, not an unwelcome interruption.

Viral Marketing (The Grand Spectacle):

Barnum was the original master of the viral stunt. He would march his elephants through town on their way to the circus tent, creating a spectacle that everyone would talk about. This was not just transportation; it was calculated, earned media. The modern equivalent is the viral marketing campaign.

Look at the launch video for Dollar Shave Club. It was irreverent, hilarious, and spoke directly to the customer in a way no Gillette ad ever had. It was a spectacle that people *chose* to share. Similarly, Liquid Death's "Murder Your Thirst" campaign uses heavy metal aesthetics and outrageous humor to make canned water the most talked-about beverage on the market. These companies didn't just advertise; they created an event.

The Power of Repetition: Building a Brand, Not Just an Ad

Barnum knew that a single ad was a whisper in the wind. He advocated for continuous, bold, and repeated advertising. "Keeping everlastingly at it," he called it. This is the foundation of modern brand building. In marketing, it's often said a customer needs to see or hear your message at least seven times before they take action.

This is why a multi-pronged approach is essential:

- A potential customer sees your **TikTok video**.
- Later, they see a **retargeting ad** on Facebook.
- They search for a solution and find your **blog post** on Google.
- They sign up for your **email newsletter** to get a free guide.
- They see a **testimonial** from another customer on Instagram.

None of these actions alone might close the sale. But together, they build a powerful sense of trust, familiarity, and authority. You move from being a stranger to being a recognized and reliable brand. You are "keeping everlastingly at it."

Advertising with Integrity: The Showman's Promise

Barnum was a showman, often accused of creating unnecessary spectacles in his day, but he operated on a core principle: always give people their money's worth. He might advertise a "mermaid," and what people saw might have been a clever fabrication, but it was a fascinating and well-crafted one. He promised a spectacle and he delivered a spectacle.

The lesson for the modern marketer is profound. Your advertising must be bold enough to capture attention, but your product must be good enough to retain trust. Clickbait head- lines that lead to disappointing content will destroy your reputation. Ads that promise a revolutionary product that is merely mediocre will lead to scathing reviews and customer backlash.

Your marketing makes a promise, but it's your product that provides the proof. A brilliant ad campaign might win you a single click, but only an exceptional experience will win you a customer for life. The goal isn't to execute a one-time transaction; it's to begin a long-term partnership built on earned trust. So be the entrepreneur who can capture the world's attention, and be the visionary whose work is so undeniable it commands respect. That is how you transform fleeting attention into unwavering, raving fans.

Quick Favor...

If you're getting some valuable takeaways from this book and the clarity to finally break through your profit plateau, would you kindly leave a quick review?

Your honest experience—even just one sentence—can help other business owners decide if this is the strategy guide they need.

Just can post a review on Amazon or scan the QR code below:

Examples:

"Finally understood why I was working harder but not profiting more"

"The frameworks are practical and immediately actionable"

"Shifted my entire approach from revenue obsession to profit focus"

"Best investment I've made in my business education"

Thank you so much for taking the time... and for taking your business seriously enough to build it the right way.

—SR Brown

CHAPTER 5

Be Kind to Your Customers and Build a Cult Following

"Politeness and civility are the best capital ever invested in business," Barnum wrote. To him, this was not a matter of basic courtesy, but a sound financial strategy. He observed that business owners who were gruff, selfish, and lacked compassion would inevitably fail, while those who were polite, accommodating, and kind would see their customers return again and again, even bringing their friends with them.

Often it is tempting to dismiss such advice as obvious. We have chatbots, sophisticated CRMs, and data-driven marketing funnels. Surely, kindness is a "soft skill" that takes a back- seat to efficiency, scalability, and systems.

This thinking is a catastrophic error. The kindness principle is not only relevant today; it is arguably the single most powerful competitive advantage in any modern economy. In an age where every customer carries a megaphone in their pocket (e.g., a smart-phone connected to the global square of social media) your customer's experience is your brand. Politeness and kindness are no longer just good manners; they are the essential tools for building a loyal, evangelistic, and highly profitable "cult following."

Every Customer is a Broadcaster

In Barnum's time, a dissatisfied customer might tell a dozen friends. Today, a single dissatisfied customer can tell thousands, and some-times even more. A scathing one-star review on Google, a viral take-down on TikTok, or a complaint thread on X (formerly Twitter) can inflict more damage on your reputation than a rival's entire marketing budget.

Conversely, a moment of genuine, above-and-beyond kindness can become a legendary piece of marketing content that money could never buy. The game has changed. Your customers are no longer the passive recipients of your service; they are active broadcasters of it. This new reality means customer service is not a cost center; it is your most critical marketing department.

From Transaction to Fandom

The goal is no longer mere customer satisfaction surveys. Satisfaction is the boring, forget- table middle ground. The new goal is to create fans, advocates, and evangelists. This is how you build a "moat" around your business that competitors cannot cross. They can copy your features, they can match your price, but they cannot replicate a genuine emotional connection with your customers.

This is achieved by operationalizing kindness. Consider the playbook used by companies famous for their cult-like followings:

Zappos (The Power of Empowerment):
The online shoe retailer built its brand not on shoes, but on legendary customer service. They famously empowered their service agents to do whatever it took to make a customer happy, with no scripts and no time limits on calls. This led to stories of agents sending flowers, ordering pizzas for customers, and overnighting free shoes to a best man who had lost his. These stories became Zappos's marketing. They weren't selling shoes; they were selling trust and kindness.

Chewy (The Art of the Personal Touch):
The online pet supply company took this a step further. They are renowned for sending hand-drawn portraits of customers' pets, handwritten holiday cards, and, most powerfully, sending flowers and a heartfelt note when they learn a customer's pet has passed away. This is not a scalable, automated process. It is a deliberate

investment in a deep, human, emotional connection. Can you measure the ROI on that bouquet of flowers? No, but it creates a customer for life and a story that will be shared with dozens of other pet owners.

Trader Joe's (Making Your People the Product):
Walk into any Trader Joe's and you'll notice the employees are not just stocking shelves; they are genuinely friendly, helpful, and seem to love their jobs. They will stop what they are doing to walk you to an item, offer you recommendations, and engage in a pleasant conversation. The "kindness" is a core part of the in-store experience. The people are as much a product as the cookie butter. Trader Joe's has built a fanatical following not just on unique products, but on the reliable promise of a pleasant human interaction.

Kindness as Your Core Strategy

How do you implement this in your own business?

1. **Hire for Empathy:** You can train for product knowledge, but you can't easily train for innate kindness. Hire people who genuinely enjoy helping others. 2. **Empower Your Front Lines:** Give your customer-facing employees the autonomy to solve problems without needing a manager's approval. Trust them to do the right thing.

3. **Look for "Surprise & Delight" Opportunities:** Systematize looking for chances to go the extra mile. A handwritten thank-you note, a small unexpected gift, or a follow-up email just to check in can transform a simple transaction into a memorable experience.

4. **Treat Your Team with Kindness:** A company that treats its employees with respect and generosity will see that kindness naturally extended to its customers.

In the end, Barnum's advice remains the bedrock of sustainable business. For the market- place increasingly dominated by algorithms and automation, genuine human kindness is the rarest and most valuable commodity of all. It is the capital that pays the highest dividends, building a fortress of loyalty that will outlast any trend, technology, or economic shift. It's the final proof that the most powerful business model isn't about ones and zeros, but about the enduring, unbreakable bond of one human being showing another that they genuinely care.

CHAPTER 6

Two Skills Entrepreneurs Must Have

The journey of an entrepreneur is not a single, heroic leap but a long, grueling marathon punctuated by unforeseen hurdles and crushing setbacks. P.T. Barnum knew this intimately. He faced devastating fires, public ridicule, and financial ruin, yet he always rebuilt. His advice on this matter was forged in the flames of his own experience and can be distilled into two powerful, intertwined commands:

Persevere, and **Do it With All Your Might.**

"Work at it, if necessary, early and late, in season and out of season," he urged, "not leaving a stone unturned, and never deferring for a single hour that which can be done just as well now." This is the doctrine of persistence. But it was coupled with a second, equally important rule: "Whatever is worth doing at all, is worth doing well." This is the doctrine of focus and excellence.

Barnum's call to persevere is what psychologist Angela Duckworth calls **Grit**. His demand to do it with all your might is what author Cal Newport has termed **Deep Work**. For the modern founder, mastering these twin disciplines is the key to transforming ambition into achievement.

Cultivating Grit

Grit is the engine that keeps you going when inspiration fades, when your initial funding runs low, and when your first (or fifth) launch fails to meet expectations. Duckworth defines it as the tendency to apply passion and perseverance to long-term goals. It is stamina. It is living life like a marathon, not a sprint.

Entrepreneurial success stories are filled with stories of grit. James Dyson famously created 5,126 failed prototypes before he perfected his first bagless vacuum cleaner. The founders of Airbnb, unable to pay their rent, resorted to selling novelty cereal boxes named "Obama O's" and "Cap'n McCain's" to keep their dream alive. These are not stories about overnight success; they are epic tales of perseverance.

In the startup mantra that celebrates "failing fast," how do you know when to persevere? A smart pivot means abandoning a bad idea. But abandoning a great one just because the path is difficult is a failure of will. Your grit is the instinct that tells you whether you've hit a dead end or just a very steep hill.

How to cultivate grit:

1. **Reframe Failure as Tuition:** Every failed experiment, every rejected pitch, every bug-filled release is not a verdict on your worth. It is data you should use to inform your decisions. It is a lesson you have paid for with time and resources. The gritty entrepreneur doesn't say, "I failed"; they say, "I learned." They are relentless in reframing failure as success.

2. **Connect to a Deeper Purpose:** Passion is what gets you started; purpose is what sees you through. To find it, you must ask the big questions: Why does this work matter beyond the bottom line? Who am I genuinely trying to help? When your "why" is more compelling than the obstacle in front of you, you unlock a new level of resilience. This purpose becomes your North Star, a fixed point in a spinning world that always reminds you which way to go.

3. **Find Your Endurance Pace:** Barnum's "early and late, in season and out of season" is not a call for burnout. A marathon runner who sprints the first mile will collapse before the finish line. Grit involves understanding your own rhythms of work and recovery. It's about building sustainable habits that allow you to remain in the game for the long haul.

The Battle for Focus: Mastering Deep Work

If grit is the engine, deep work is the transmission that channels that power into forward motion. Cal Newport defines Deep Work as "professional activities performed in a state of distraction-free concentration that push your cognitive capabilities to their limit." This is the work that creates new value, solves hard problems, and produces things that are difficult to replicate. It is the opposite of **Shallow Work**: the low-value, logistical tasks like answering emails, attending status meetings, and responding to Slack notifications that consume the majority of the modern professional's day.

Barnum's command to do things "with all your might" was a warning against the dangers of shallow, half-hearted effort. In his era, the primary distraction might have been town gossip. In ours, it is a ceaseless digital barrage from a thousand different apps and inboxes, all engineered to steal your most valuable resource: your attention.

The ability to shut out the noise and concentrate deeply is a superpower in any economy. The founder who can spend three hours in uninterrupted focus developing a core business strategy will outperform the founder who spends those same three hours reacting to a flood of distractions.

How to master deep work:

1. **Schedule Concentration Like an Appointment:** Do not wait for focus to find you. Block out "deep work" sessions on your calendar. Treat them with the same respect as a meeting with your most important investor. During this time, all notifications are off, all unnecessary browser tabs are closed, and you are completely unavailable to the outside world.

2. **Create a Sanctuary:** Designate a physical space or a set of rituals that signal to your brain it is time to focus. This could be a specific room, a pair of noise canceling headphones, or a particular type of music. The goal is to create a distraction-free environment void of external stimuli.

3. **Embrace Productive Boredom:** Our brains have been trained to seek constant attention. We reflexively pull out our

phones at the first hint of boredom. To regain your ability to concentrate, you must break this habit. Allow yourself to be bored. Go for walks without your phone. Let your mind wander. This practice rebuilds the mental muscles required for sustained, deep focus.

Grit without deep work is just ineffective busy work. Deep work without grit is a series of passion-fueled but unfinished projects. The successful entrepreneur marries the two. They have the long-term vision and resilience to weather the storms, and the disciplined focus to do the difficult, high-value work required to turn that vision into a reality. This is how you leave no stone unturned. This is how you do it with all your might.

CHAPTER 7

Don't Get Above Your Business: Stay Lean, Agile, and Connected

There is a subtle poison that can infect an entrepreneur, and it is most potent at the moment of first success. After the struggle and sacrifice, when the revenue starts to flow and the team begins to grow, a dangerous temptation arises: the temptation to float "above" the business. During his time, Barnum witnessed occasions when young merchants achieved a degree of success, then felt they were suddenly too important for the daily grind. "They began to feel they were 'somebody,' and could now afford to take it easy." This, he warned, was the beginning of the end.

This perfectly describes the actions that often kills inexperienced entrepreneurs. The founder who gets "above their business" is the one who stops talking to customers, stops using their own product, and loses touch with the core operations that created their success in the first place. The modern antidote to this poison is a powerful combination of methodologies and mindsets: staying **Lean**, being **Agile**, and remaining obsessively **Connected** to your customers and your team.

The Agile Mindset

The "waterfall" leader is the founder who develops a grand vision in isolation, hands a 100- page plan or specification document to their team, and expects a perfect product to be delivered within a certain time period. This approach is arrogant and incredibly risky because it assumes the founder's initial vision is flawless and that the market will remain static.

The Agile methodology is the direct counter-argument. It insists that value is created iteratively and collaboratively. Instead of grand, time-phased plans, work is done in short "sprints." Instead of rigid specifications, the team works from a flexible backlog or list of prioritized task. This process forces the founder to stay engaged. You cannot be "above" a business that operates on a two-week cycle of building, testing, and learning. You must be in the trenches with your team, making trade-offs, reviewing progress, and constantly re-evaluating priorities based on real-world feedback. An agile founder cannot afford the luxury of detachment; the system demands their presence and participation.

"Get Out of the Building": The Lean Imperative

"A man should know his business from A to Z," Barnum insisted, and knowing your customer from A to Z is what it looks like today. The Lean Startup methodology, pioneered by Eric Ries and Steve Blank, is built on this principle. Its central mantra is a direct command to avoid getting above your business: **"Get out of the building."**

You cannot understand your customers' problems from the comfort of your corner office. You cannot grasp their frustrations by reading a summary report prepared by your marketing team. You must seek out the messy, unvarnished truth for yourself. This means:

Conducting the interviews yourself: In the early days, the founder must be the one talking to potential users, listening to their problems, and learning their language.

Watching them use your product: You will learn more from silently observing a user struggle with your interface for five minutes than you will from a dozen internal meetings.

Answering the support tickets: Founders of wildly successful companies like Slack and Basecamp were famous for spending time on the front lines of customer support. It kept them viscerally connected to the user experience and provided a raw, unfiltered stream of feedback for product improvement.

Staying lean means staying grounded in the reality of your customer's experience. The moment you believe you are too important for this work is the moment your product starts to diverge from what the market actually needs.

Staying Connected Through Data

A founder who is "above their business" relies on vanity metrics—superficial numbers like app downloads or social media followers that feel good but signify little. A connected founder, by contrast, is fluent in the language of their business's true health. They are obsessed with the metrics that matter:

- **Customer Acquisition Cost (CAC):** How much does it really cost to get a new customer?
- **Lifetime Value (LTV):** How much is that customer worth over time?
- **Churn Rate:** How quickly are we losing customers?
- **Engagement Metrics:** Are people actually *using* the features we are building?

Here are the calculations for each metric:
CUSTOMER ACQUISITION COST (CAC)
Formula:

Total Sales & Marketing Costs ÷ Number of New Customers Acquired Calculation:

CAC = (Sales team salaries + Marketing spend +

Advertising costs + Tools/so=ware + Commissions) ÷ New customers

Example:
- Monthly marketing spend: $50,000
- New customers acquired: 500
- CAC = $50,000 ÷ 500 = $100 per customer

LIFETIME VALUE (LTV)
Formula:

Average Revenue Per Customer × Gross Margin × (1 ÷ Churn Rate)

Calculation:
LTV = Monthly Revenue per Customer × Gross Margin % × (1 ÷ Monthly Churn Rate)

Example:
- Monthly revenue per customer: $50
- Gross margin: 80%
- Monthly churn rate: 5%
- LTV = $50 × 0.80 × (1 ÷ 0.05) = $50 × 0.80 × 20 = $800

CHURN RATE
Formula:

(Customers Lost During Period ÷ Total Customers at Start of Period) × 100 Calculation:
Monthly Churn = (Customers who canceled this month ÷ Customers at beginning of month) × 100

Example:
- Customers at start of month: 1,000
- Customers who canceled: 50
- Churn Rate = (50 ÷ 1,000) × 100 = 5%

ENGAGEMENT METRICS

Daily Active Users (DAU):

$$DAU = \text{Unique users who performed key action in last 24 hours}$$

Monthly Active Users (MAU):

$$MAU = \text{Unique users who performed key action in last 30 days}$$

Feature Adoption Rate:

$$\text{Feature Adoption} = (\text{Users who used feature} \div \text{Total users}) \times 100$$

User Engagement Score:

$$\text{Engagement Score} = (DAU \div MAU) \times 100$$

Example:
- DAU: 2,000 users
- MAU: 10,000 users
- Engagement Score = (2,000 ÷ 10,000) × 100 = 20%

. . .

HEALTHY BENCHMARKS:
- LTV should be 3-5x higher than CAC
- Monthly churn should be <5% for most businesses
- Engagement score >20% is generally strong

These benchmarks are dependent upon the industry, and you should definitely do research so that you know what are healthy benchmarks for the industry that you're in.

This data is the objective truth-teller. It cuts through optimistic projections and office politics. A founder who is deeply engaged with their core metrics can never float too far from reality. The numbers keep them anchored to the actual performance of the business, forcing hard questions and honest assessments long before a crisis becomes irreversible.

Ultimately, humility is the core discipline. It is the understanding that you, the founder, serve the business and its customers, not the other way around. Humility keeps you curious. It keeps you listening. It ensures you are never too proud to do the work that matters, whether that's interviewing a user, debugging a line of code, or analyzing a spreadsheet. The business and customers that made you a success still needs you in the trenches. Don't get above it.

Your Reputation Is Your Most Valuable Asset

Of all the forms of capital an entrepreneur can secure (e.g., financial, intellectual, social), P.T. Barnum believed "the best kind of capital is a good character." To him, a reputation built on honesty and integrity was more powerful than a vault full of gold. A person known for their integrity could lose everything such as, money, property, and business, and still retain the power to rise again. Their reputation becomes their greatest asset, opening doors that remain forever closed to those who have squandered their credibility. Trust, once earned, becomes the foundation for every future opportunity.

In a world obsessed with growth hacking, disruption, and the relentless pursuit of unicorn valuations, a focus on simple, old-fashioned integrity can seem hopelessly idealistic. But it is the most vital and strategic principle of all. Deceptive shortcuts, ethically dubious tactics, and a "fake it 'til you make it" ethos might create a temporary illusion of success, but they plant the seeds of certain collapse. With the constant pursuit for authenticity, your reputation is not just a part of your business; it is the foundation upon which your entire business success rests.

The Glass House Economy: Honesty as a Tactical Imperative

Your business today operates inside a glass house. Every action, every customer interaction, every internal memo has the potential to be broadcast to the world in an instant. A dissatisfied customer's tweet, a disgruntled employee's Glassdoor review, or a leaked video from an internal meeting; these are the modern forces that hold businesses to account.

This new reality means honesty and integrity are no longer simply moral choices; they are a must. You cannot create a company built with smoke and mirrors and expect it to survive. The public will eventually look behind the curtain, and when they do, the backlash will be swift and brutal.

Consider the cautionary tale of Fyre Festival. Its promoters used slick marketing, celebrity influencers, and grandiose promises to build immense hype. They sold a dream. But the dream was a lie, built on a foundation of deceit. When the truth was revealed, not by investigative journalists at first, but by the attendees themselves in real-time on social media, the collapse was instantaneous and cringe-worthy. The brand became a global punchline overnight, a permanent digital monument to the punishment that comes from promising what you cannot deliver.

Your Reputation is Your Permanent Record

Think of it this way: In Barnum's time, a reputation was built on memory. Today, it's built on receipts. The internet keeps a permanent, searchable record of every promise you've kept and every one you've broken. Your integrity isn't just a feeling people have about you; it's a trail of digital evidence (customer reviews, Glassdoor ratings, social media comments) that tells the undeniable story of your character. The pros and cons of your reputation is quantifiable. Your integrity, or lack thereof, can be etched into the digital bedrock of Google search results, online reviews, and social media archives.

A positive reputation is the most powerful marketing engine you can build. It is the cumulative effect of thousands of small acts of integrity: meeting deadlines, honoring warranties, handling complaints with grace, and treating employees with respect. This creates a moat of trust around your business that is nearly impossible for competitors to breach.

A negative reputation, however, is a debt that compounds. A single scandal, a pattern of poor reviews, or an ethical breach can become an anchor that drags down your business forever. Every potential customer, investor, and employee will Google you. If the first page of results is dominated by stories of bad service, operational failures, and questionable ethics, you are, in business terms, already dead.

This is the lesson of Theranos. Elizabeth Holmes was a master of Barnum-esque showmanship, crafting a compelling story of revolutionizing healthcare. But it was a narrative built on a fundamental deception. The technology did not work. For years, she maintained the illusion through secrecy and intimidation. But when the truth finally emerged, the entire multi-billion-dollar edifice imploded. Her reputation was not just tarnished; it was annihilated, becoming a permanent case study in corporate fraud. She had all the showmanship, but none of the essential, underlying integrity.

Building a Business That Stands for Something

The modern definition of integrity extends beyond mere honesty in transactions. It now encompasses a company's total impact on the world. Consumers and, most critically, top-tier talent are increasingly drawn to businesses that are a force for good. This is the heart of "Conscious Capitalism"—the idea that businesses can be both profitable and purposeful.

This is where integrity gets real. It's about seeking honest answers to the hard questions:

- How do you treat your lowest-paid employee?
- What is your supply chain's impact on the environment?
- Do you contribute positively to the communities you operate in?
- Do you build products that genuinely improve people's lives?

Patagonia is the gold standard for business integrity. Their commitment to environmental sustainability is not a marketing slogan; it is woven into the very fabric of their operations, from the materials they source to their "Don't Buy This Jacket" ad campaigns that encourage mindful consumption. This unwavering integrity has earned them a fanatically loyal customer base and the ability to attract passionate, mission-driven employees. Their brand is built on a reputation so solid that it has become its most valuable asset.

Ultimately, preserving your integrity is the ultimate long-term strategy. It is the under- standing that how you make your money is more important than how much you make. Every decision, every interaction, every product launch is a brick in the structure of your reputation. Build it with honesty, fairness, and a genuine desire to provide value, and you will have constructed a fortress that can withstand any storm. Neglect it, and you are building on sand, waiting for the inevitable tide.

Focus Your Efforts

The modern entrepreneur lives in a candy store of opportunity. A new social media platform emerges, promising a new audience. A new technology trend appears, hinting at a new market. The allure of the "side hustle" and "multiple streams of income" is a constant whisper. In the face of this endless buffet of possibilities, one of P.T. Barnum's sternest warnings was **"do not scatter your powers."**

"Engage in one kind of business only, and stick to it faithfully," Barnum advised, "until you succeed, or until your experience shows that you should abandon it." He saw countless promising individuals fail for one reason: they divided their energy. They would get a good business going, only to be distracted by a speculative oil well or a "wonderful" invention, siphoning time, capital, and focus away from their core enterprise until everything collapsed.

This is the classic, fatal trap of **Shiny Object Syndrome**. The energy that should be a focused, powerful laser beam, capable of cutting through steel, becomes a weak, diffused light, accomplishing nothing. The capital that could have funded market dominance is spread thin across a portfolio of mediocrity. The focus that could have created a world-class product is fractured among a dozen half-finished projects.

The High Cost of Divided Attention

Imagine a young SaaS company finally achieving product-market fit. Their core software is gaining traction. But then the founder gets distracted. They decide the company also needs to launch a daily podcast, build a complex consulting arm, and start a merchandise line, all at the same time.

What happens? The core product, the very engine of their success, stops getting the attention it needs. Bug fixes slow down. Key feature development stalls. Meanwhile, the podcast is inconsistent, the consulting clients are underserved, and the t-shirts aren't selling. They have abandoned their pursuit of being world-class at one thing to become amateur-class at four things. They have scattered their powers, and failure becomes a self-fulfilling prophecy.

This is not just about time management; it's about cognitive load. Building one successful business requires your full, obsessive attention. Juggling two or more unrelated ventures means you are never fully present or focused on any of them.

Master Your Core Business First

The modern mantra should be: **Mastery before multiplicity.** The great empires of business were not built by diversifying on day one. They were built by achieving absolute dominance in a single, focused area.

Amazon began by doing one thing: selling books online. For years, Jeff Bezos relentlessly focused on becoming the best bookseller in the world. Only after achieving market dominance and building a powerful logistical backbone did he begin to methodically expand into other categories.

Starbucks focused for decades on a singular mission: creating the "third place" between work and home by perfecting the premium coffee shop experience. They didn't try to also become a bakery and a lunch spot and a merchandise giant all at once. Those additions came later, as natural extensions of a masterfully executed core business.

The lesson is clear: Earn your right to diversify. The freedom and resources that come from a wildly successful primary business are what make secondary ventures possible. Chasing them prematurely is how you guarantee you achieve neither.

The Exception: The Power of Adjacency

Barnum did offer one crucial exception to his rule. It is acceptable to engage in ventures that are directly related to, and supportive of, your main business. This is the principle of **Adjacency**.

A successful software company that sells to marketers might logically start a conference for marketers. The conference strengthens the core business by building community, generating leads, and reinforcing the brand's authority. This is not a distraction; it is a strategic fortification.

The key question to ask when considering a new opportunity is: *Does this directly strengthen our core mission?*

A fitness studio starting a line of branded athletic apparel? **Yes.**

The same fitness studio trying to develop a cryptocurrency trading app? **No.**

Learning to distinguish between a strategic adjacency and a shiny object distraction is a critical skill for any founder. The discipline to say "no" to a hundred good ideas is what allows you to say "yes" to the one great one.

Preserve your focus as your most sacred resource. Go deep, not wide. Pour all your energy and talent into making one thing exceptional. Master it. Dominate it. And you will have earned the right to do anything else you choose.

CHAPTER 10

Summary

Most entrepreneurs are solving the wrong problem. They obsess over funding, market timing, and the latest growth hacks while ignoring the foundational principles that actually build wealth. The result? Ninety percent of startups fail within their first year, not because they lack good ideas, but because they lack the timeless strategies that separate lasting success from fleeting trends.

This Unstoppable Profit for Business Owners is an entrepreneur money making playbook that reveals the battle-tested blueprint hidden in plain sight: part of the 15 operational principles that P.T. Barnum used to build a $300 million fortune (in today's dollars) not once, but three times—recovering from complete financial ruin twice. Barnum pioneered viral marketing before the concept existed. He invented FOMO through scarcity and urgency, mastered the art of customer experience design, and built the first truly global personal brand.

Most importantly, Barnum faced the exact same entrepreneurial battles most of us entrepreneurs face today: sleepless nights wondering if his product would find its market, the crushing weight of payroll when revenue dipped, the constant fight for attention in a crowded marketplace, and the temptation to chase every shiny opportunity that crossed his path. His solutions weren't magic—they were methodical, repeatable principles that work as powerfully today as they did 150 years ago.

The Core Problem: Founder-Market Mismatch

The insight in this book challenges conventional startup wisdom. While most entrepreneurs focus on achieving Product-Market Fit first, this approach is backwards. You need Founder Market Fit before you can achieve sustainable Product-Market Fit. This means aligning your unique zone of genius with genuine market opportunity and authentic passion. This same principle drove Barnum's transformation from a failed shopkeeper into an unstoppable showman. His genius wasn't in quiet behind-the-scenes sales—it was in spectacular promotion and public attention. The moment he aligned his natural talents with market demand, he became unstoppable.

The Modern Translation: Timeless Principles, New Applications

Barnum's principles translate directly to today's entrepreneurial challenges, but with modern tools and contexts. Where he competed for attention on crowded city streets, you compete in crowded social media feeds. Where he had to overcome skepticism about his "curiosities," you must overcome skepticism about your startup's bold claims. Where he needed systems to manage a traveling circus with hundreds of employees, you need systems to scale a remote team across time zones.

The book demonstrates how these principles power today's most successful companies. Amazon's relentless focus on customer obsession mirrors Barnum's belief that "politeness and civility are the best capital ever invested in business." Patagonia's unwavering commitment to environmental integrity exemplifies Barnum's warning that "the best kind of capital is a good character." The Dollar Shave Club's viral growth strategy echoes Barnum's mastery of creating spectacles that people choose to share.

The Strategic Framework

Rather than chasing trends or copying competitors, the book provides a systematic approach to building wealth through three critical phases. First, establish your foundation by finding your founder-market fit, choosing strategic locations (both digital and physical), and mastering smart capital, understanding the difference between debt that serves you and debt that keeps you limited. Second, engineer sustainable growth by capturing attention authentically, creating customer evangelists rather than mere customers, developing unbreakable persistence, staying connected to your core business operations, and building an unassailable reputation in an age where integrity is both a moral imperative and a tactical advantage. Third, achieve systematic scale by maintaining laser focus on your core business, avoiding the fatal trap of "shiny object syndrome," and creating systems that work without you.

The Ultimate Competitive Advantage

The book's most powerful insight is that in an age of algorithms, automation, and artificial intelligence, the timeless human elements —integrity, persistence, genuine customer care, and focused execution—become the ultimate competitive advantages. While competitors chase the latest marketing tactics or growth hacks, entrepreneurs who master these foundational principles build businesses that compound wealth over decades rather than months.

Barnum's legacy isn't just entertainment—it's a complete system for turning vision into wealth. His principles survived the Industrial Revolution, the Information Age, and now the AI Revolution because they're based on unchanging human psychology and sound business fundamentals. The tools change, but the principles remain constant.

The Entrepreneur Money Making Playbook doesn't just tell inspiring stories—it provides the precise, actionable framework that transforms ambitious ideas into money making enterprises. Whether you're launching a tech startup, opening a local business, or scaling an existing company, these 15 principles provide the roadmap to build real wealth while creating something meaningful that changes the world.

One Last Thing...

If this book gave you the clarity and momentum to finally break through your profit plateau, would you kindly leave a quick review?

Your honest experience—even just one sentence—can help other business owners decide if this is the strategy guide they need.

Just scan to review on Amazon:

Examples:

- "Finally understood why I was working harder but not profiting more"
- "The frameworks are practical and immediately actionable"
- "Shifted my entire approach from revenue obsession to profit focus"
- "Best investment I've made in my business education"

Thank you so much for taking the time... and for taking your business seriously enough to build it the right way.

—SR Brown

P.S. READY TO take your profit engine to the next level?

Now that you've reviewed the profit foundations in this book, discover how to leverage critical business strategies to build wealth and scale your business.

Check out ***How To Make Money In Business Online***

which shows you exactly how to build sustainable online revenue streams—whether you're adding digital products to your existing business or going fully online.

Because offline profit creates stability. Online profit creates scale.

Available now on Amazon: **Get It Here**

9 789899 276797